M000306021
LOUP GAROU

**Author:** Moon / **Illustrator:** 2D / **Translation:** JF Gagné
This book is a translation of the original *Loup Garou* © Makaka Éditions


ISBN : 978-0-9997698-2-9 Library of Congress Control Number: 2018933575

Published by Van Ryder Games and printed in the USA. Second printing.

Find printable character sheets and the entire collection of Graphic Novel Adventures at **www.vanrydergames.com**

DREADHORN COUNTY, TOWN OF WHITETHORN.

WHILE MOST OF ITS INHABITANTS ARE ALREADY FAST ASLEEP...

HOLY ROASTED TROLL RUMP!
THE OLD MAGE THEDOCRED AND HIS APPRENTICE EORAS ARE STILL WORKING!

PROBLEM, MASTER?

IT IS A DISASTER, A CATASTROPHE, A CALAMITY!

THAT BAD?

YES! MUCH WORSE EVEN THAN THAT TIME WHEN I INADVERTENTLY TRANSFORMED YOU INTO A FROG.

WE'RE OUT OF THREE-EYED SLUG SLIME. NOT EVEN A SINGLE DROP!

WITHOUT IT, I CANNOT COMPLETE THE WART-BLASTER OINTMENT I MUST SELL AT THE MARKET TOMORROW. WHAT WILL I DO?

BUT MASTER, COULDN'T WE USE YOUNG MANDRAGORA LEAVES INSTEAD?

ACCORDING TO YOUR NOTES, THEY ARE JUST AS POTENT. BESIDES, I BELIEVE I SAW SOME IN THE FOREST THIS MORNING.

MY YOUNG APPRENTICE, YOU ARE A GENIUS! NOW, COVER UP WELL. IT IS COLD OUTSIDE!

I MUST... GO... NOW?

EORAS! IF YOU SEE SOME CENTAURS, WOULD YOU MIND BRINGING BACK A FEW HAIRS FROM THEIR MANE FOR ME?!
ERR... OF COURSE, MASTER!
AND DON'T VENTURE INTO THE SWAMPS! THEY'RE DANGEROUS THIS TIME OF YEAR!

I'VE BEEN HAD ONCE AGAIN, IT SEEMS...

YOU ARE NOW EXITING THE PEACEFUL TOWN OF WHITETHORN. WE WISH YOU SAFE TRAVELS AND HOPE TO SEE YOU VERY SOON... IN ONE PIECE!
COURAGE EORAS. IN A FEW MINUTES, ALL OF THIS WILL BE OVER AND YOU'LL GO BACK TO THE COMFORT OF YOUR COZY BED!

I AM NOT AFRAID.
I AM NOT AFRAID-

GRRRRRRRRR !!!

WHO'S THERE? COME OUT OF THE SHADOWS!

BY THE GODDESS IGOTH, THAT'S... A *LOUP GAROU*... A WEREWOLF!

I'VE GOT YOU!

HELP ME!

THAT WAS A CLOSE ONE! WHOEVER YOU ARE, THANK YOU!

LUCKILY, THE WEREWOLF DID NOT BITE ME! AND TO THINK, I COULD HAVE BECOME A *LOUP GAROU!*

HOLD ON, THE FULL MOON IS NOT EVEN OUT TONIGHT.
VERY OBSERVANT OF YOU! THESE MONSTERS HAVE FOUND A WAY TO TRANSFORM WHENEVER THEY DESIRE. FORTUNATELY, I AM HERE TO REMIND THEM THAT THE FOREST DOES NOT BELONG TO THEM.

THANK YOU KINDLY SIR, IT IS REASSURING TO KNOW THERE ARE WEREWOLF HUNTERS IN WHITETHORN. THANKS TO YOU, WE NO LONGER HAVE TO FEAR THEIR ATTACKS! ALLOW ME TO INTRODUCE MYSELF: MY NAME IS EORAS. I AM THE APPRENTICE OF...

....OH NO!

I KNOW WHAT YOU ARE. DON'T MOVE!

YOU NOW PLAY THE ROLE OF EORAS, MAGE APPRENTICE AND, HEREAFTER, A YOUNG *LOUP GAROU*: A WEREWOLF!

THE MAN WHO SAVED YOUR LIFE A FEW MINUTES EARLIER IS NOW POINTING A CROSSBOW AT YOU. YOUR PULSE ACCELERATES AS YOU RECOGNIZE HIM. THE MAN STANDING BEFORE YOU IS SALANDAR, THE FAMOUS WEREWOLF HUNTER.

BEFORE FLEEING TO PANEL 1, READ THE FOLLOWING RULES AND WRITE THE INFORMATION LISTED HERE ON YOUR CHARACTER SHEET, FOUND IN THE BACK OF THIS BOOK ON PAGES 141/142!

EORAS, HUMAN FORM:

HIT POINTS: 10
MAGIC POINTS: 10
STRENGTH: 4
DEFENSE: 1
GOLD PIECES (GP): 20
1 SKILL POINT TO SPEND

# Rules of Play

## DEAR ADVENTURER,

YOU ARE NOW PLAYING EORAS, THE MAGE APPRENTICE, WHO HAS JUST BECOME A WEREWOLF, OR *LOUP GAROU*, AT THE BEGINNING OF THE STORY.

YOUR GOAL IS VERY SIMPLE: SURVIVE.

YOU'LL HAVE TO ESCAPE FROM SALANDAR, THE HUNTER. TO ACCOMPLISH THIS, YOU WILL RUN THROUGH THE FOREST WHERE ADVENTURE AWAITS! ALWAYS KEEP YOUR EYES OPEN, FOR SOME PATHS ARE HIDDEN!

FIND THE CHARACTER SHEET ON PAGE 141. WE INVITE YOU TO REMOVE IT FROM THE BOOK OR DOWNLOAD A COPY OF IT ON WWW.VANRYDERGAMES.COM UNDER THE GAME'S ENTRY. GIVE EORAS A TITLE OR NICKNAME, WHATEVER YOU PREFER. FOR EXAMPLE, 'EORAS, ARCANE MASTER' OR 'EORAS, DARKSTALKER.'

ON YOUR WAY, YOU WILL HAVE OPPORTUNITIES TO COLLECT GOLD PIECES (GP) AND ITEMS, PROVIDED THAT YOU CAN CARRY THEM OF COURSE (FOR EXAMPLE, IT IS IMPOSSIBLE TO CARRY A COW OR AN ANVIL). YOU WILL NEED TO SPOT SOME HIDDEN ITEMS ON YOUR OWN AND WILL NOT BE PROMPTED BY GAME TEXT TO TAKE THEM. YOU BEGIN THE STORY WITH A TEN-SLOT BAG. EACH TIME YOU TAKE AN ITEM, MAKE NOTE OF IT IN YOUR INVENTORY ON YOUR CHARACTER SHEET.

SOME ITEMS MUST BE EQUIPPED (A PAIR OF GLOVES, A COAT, A WEAPON, ETC.), MAKE A NOTE OF IT ON YOUR CHARACTER SHEET IN THE APPROPRIATE PLACE IN THE "EQUIPMENT" SECTION (EQUIPPED ITEMS DO NOT TAKE UP AN INVENTORY SLOT, BUT YOU MAY ONLY EQUIP ONE ITEM OF EACH TYPE).

YOU HAVE TWO ATTRIBUTES: STRENGTH AND DEFENSE. DO NOT FORGET TO WRITE THE STARTING VALUES FROM PAGE 7 ON YOUR CHARACTER SHEET. STRENGTH IS USED IN MELEE COMBATS WITH WEAPONS; DEFENSE IS YOUR CAPACITY TO DEFEND YOURSELF IN COMBAT. WHEN YOU TURN INTO YOUR WEREWOLF FORM, YOU WILL GAIN +5 STRENGTH AND +5 DEFENSE. THESE BONUSES WILL BE LOST WHEN YOU CHANGE BACK INTO YOUR HUMAN FORM.

IN THE "EXPERIENCE POINTS" SECTION OF YOUR CHARACTER SHEET, YOU WILL FIND MANY SQUARES. EACH OF THESE SQUARES REPRESENTS ONE EXPERIENCE POINT OR XP. FOR SHORT.

THESE XP ARE GAINED WHEN YOU WIN A BATTLE OR SOLVE A RIDDLE.

AS SOON AS YOU'VE FILLED EVERY SQUARE IN A SECTION, YOU HAVE GONE UP A LEVEL AND GAIN 1 HIT POINT AND 1 MAGIC POINT.

EACH TIME YOU GO UP A LEVEL, AS WELL AS AT THE BEGINNING OF THE GAME, YOU GAIN 1 SKILL POINT. THESE POINTS ALLOW YOU TO UNLOCK THE SKILLS FOUND ON THE BACK OF YOUR CHARACTER SHEET. DURING YOUR ADVENTURE, THEY WILL ALLOW YOU TO SPECIALIZE IN A PROFESSION OF YOUR CHOICE. TO CHOOSE A PROFESSION, USE A SKILL POINT TO FILL IN THE FIRST (LOWEST) BOX. YOU MAY BEGIN A NEW PROFESSION ANY TIME, BUT SPECIALIZING WILL LEAD TO MORE POWERFUL SKILLS. YOUR DESTINY IS IN YOUR HANDS!

YOU HAVE NOW LEARNED THE RULES YOU NEED TO KNOW TO BEGIN YOUR ADVENTURE.

SOON, YOU WILL LEARN HOW TO TURN INTO A WEREWOLF AND HOW TO ENGAGE IN COMBAT FOR WHICH YOU WILL NEED THE DISC AT THE BACK OF THIS BOOK. ALTERNATIVELY, YOU MAY INSTEAD USE A SIX-SIDED DIE (NOT INCLUDED) ANY TIME YOU ARE ASKED TO SPIN THE DISC .

1.

FOREST
SWAMP
216
136

2.

276
19
76

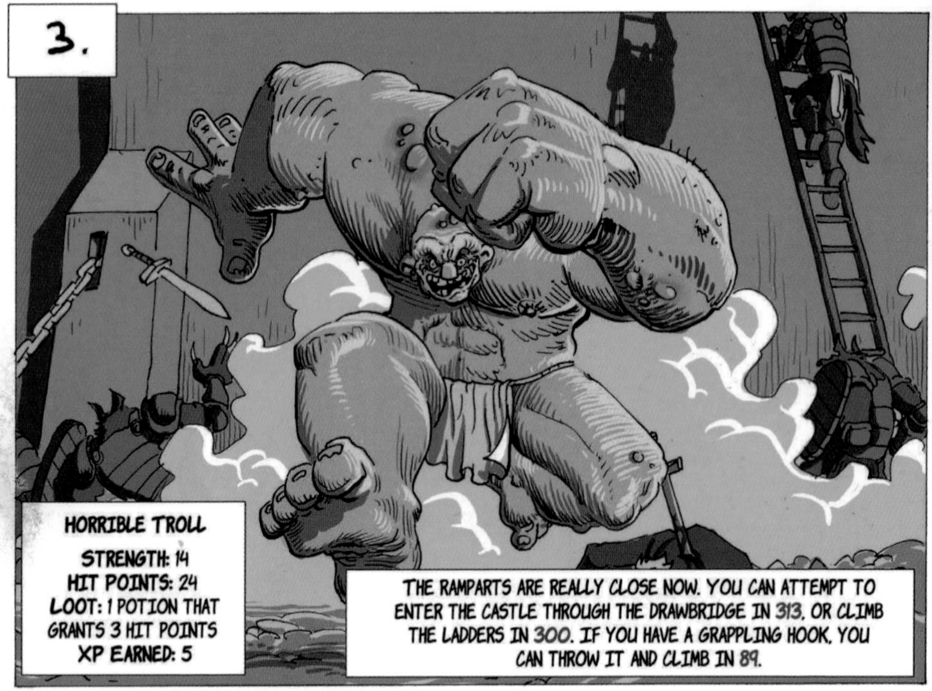

3.

HORRIBLE TROLL

STRENGTH: 14
HIT POINTS: 24
LOOT: 1 POTION THAT GRANTS 3 HIT POINTS
XP EARNED: 5

THE RAMPARTS ARE REALLY CLOSE NOW. YOU CAN ATTEMPT TO ENTER THE CASTLE THROUGH THE DRAWBRIDGE IN 313, OR CLIMB THE LADDERS IN 300. IF YOU HAVE A GRAPPLING HOOK, YOU CAN THROW IT AND CLIMB IN 89.

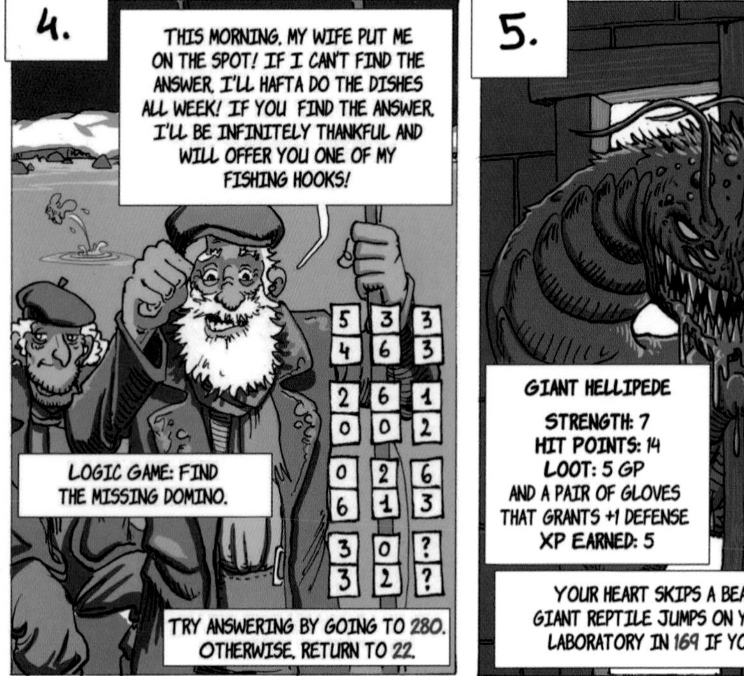
4.
THIS MORNING, MY WIFE PUT ME ON THE SPOT! IF I CAN'T FIND THE ANSWER, I'LL HAFTA DO THE DISHES ALL WEEK! IF YOU FIND THE ANSWER, I'LL BE INFINITELY THANKFUL AND WILL OFFER YOU ONE OF MY FISHING HOOKS!
5 4 | 3 6 | 3 3
2 0 | 6 0 | 1 2
0 6 | 2 1 | 6 3
3 3 | 0 2 | ? ?
LOGIC GAME: FIND THE MISSING DOMINO.
TRY ANSWERING BY GOING TO 280. OTHERWISE, RETURN TO 22.
5.
GIANT HELLIPEDE
STRENGTH: 7
HIT POINTS: 14
LOOT: 5 GP AND A PAIR OF GLOVES THAT GRANTS +1 DEFENSE
XP EARNED: 5
YOUR HEART SKIPS A BEAT WHEN THIS GIANT REPTILE JUMPS ON YOU! GO TO THE LABORATORY IN 169 IF YOU DEFEAT IT!

6.

HER PULSE IS WEAK BUT SHE'LL SURVIVE!

INFURIATED, YOU HOWL IN ANGER AND DASH BACK TO 240! THERE IS NO TIME TO LOSE! THEDOCRED MAY ALSO BE DYING!

7.

HERE YOU ARE IN FRONT OF THE OLD LIBRARY. THOUGH IT WAS ABANDONED MANY YEARS AGO, YOUR LUPINE HEARING PICKS UP THE SOUND OF VOICES INSIDE. YOUR HEART IS POUNDING... ARE YOU READY TO FACE OFF AGAINST VAMPIRES? IF YOU DO NOT YET HAVE THE MEANS TO TRANSFORM INTO A WEREWOLF AT WILL, GO BACK TO TOWN IN 180.
IF YOU CAN, TRANSFORM FOR 1 HIT POINT AND ENTER IN 119.

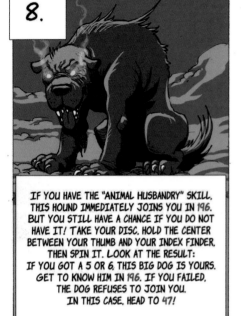

8.
IF YOU HAVE THE "ANIMAL HUSBANDRY" SKILL, THIS HOUND IMMEDIATELY JOINS YOU IN 196. BUT YOU STILL HAVE A CHANCE IF YOU DO NOT HAVE IT! TAKE YOUR DISC, HOLD THE CENTER BETWEEN YOUR THUMB AND YOUR INDEX FINDER, THEN SPIN IT. LOOK AT THE RESULT: IF YOU GOT A 5 OR 6, THIS BIG DOG IS YOURS. GET TO KNOW HIM IN 196. IF YOU FAILED, THE DOG REFUSES TO JOIN YOU. IN THIS CASE, HEAD TO 47!

9.
177

10.
YES... WHAT IS IT?
MISTER VINUS IS THE MAN YOU MET IN THE WOODS EARLIER. HE RECOGNIZES YOU AND OFFERS TO LET YOU IN AT 73. TO GO BACK TO THE STREET, RETURN TO 173.

11.
YOU'VE FALLEN IN THE MOAT AND IT IS IMPOSSIBLE FOR YOU TO RETURN TO FIRM GROUND BECAUSE OF THE BATTLE. A GOOD ALTERNATIVE IS THE DRAWBRIDGE IN 230. AS IS THE HOLE IN THE WALL IN 52.

## 12.

HORNED YETI
STRENGTH: 4
HIT POINTS: 15
LOOT: 5 GP
AND BOOTS THAT
GRANT 1 DEFENSE POINT
XP EARNED: 4
IF YOU SURVIVE THIS COMBAT, GO BACK TO 179 AFTER GRABBING YOUR LOOT. YOU CANNOT RETURN HERE.

## 13.

YOUR NEW WOLF SENSES ALLOW YOU TO SMELL THE DELICATE AROMA COMING FROM THE FISHMONGER'S STALL. YOU'RE VERY CLOSE TO THE TOWN! CONTINUE IN 120.

## 14.

JASTOK? OLDRAK? IS ANYBODY HERE? I HAVE NEWS CONCERNING THEDOCRED! THAT CRAZY OLD MAN IS WITH THE VAMPIRES!

SALANDAR! WHAT IS HE DOING HERE? WHY IS HE INTERESTED IN THEDOCRED? FEARING THAT OLDRAK MIGHT BE AROUND, YOU TAKE THE OTHER EXIT IN 141.

15.
BAG OF DARKNESS
BONUS: THIS IS A 15-SLOT BAG.
YOU'VE FOUND A BAG OF DARKNESS! IT GOES WONDERFULLY WELL WITH YOUR TUNIC. WHETHER YOU CHOOSE TO KEEP IT OR NOT, GO TO 142.

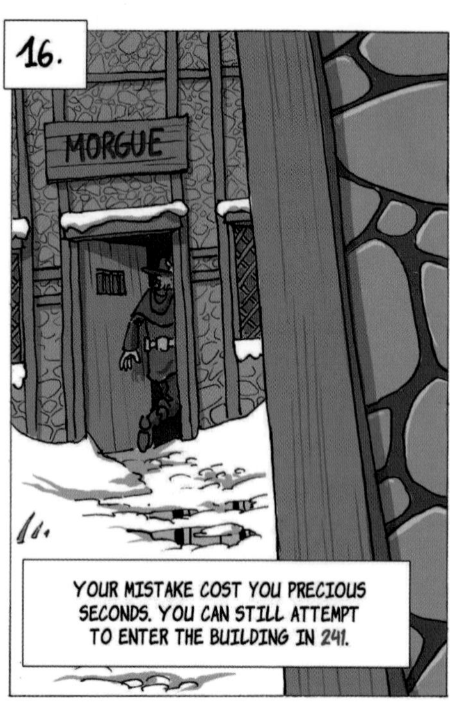
16.
MORGUE
YOUR MISTAKE COST YOU PRECIOUS SECONDS. YOU CAN STILL ATTEMPT TO ENTER THE BUILDING IN 241.

17.

221

273

18.

ANOTHER BASTARD WHO THINKS HE CAN KILL ME AND GET THE REWARD!

WHITETHORN BANDIT

STRENGTH: 8
HIT POINTS: 18
LOOT: 6 GP
AND A POTION THAT GRANTS 2 MAGIC POINTS
XP EARNED: 5

WHEN YOU RECOGNIZE THE BANDIT, YOUR HEART SKIPS A BEAT. IF YOU MANAGE TO DEFEAT HIM, YOU TAKE HIS NECKLACE IDENTIFYING HIM AS A MEMBER OF THE ASSASSIN'S GUILD. YOU WILL NEED TO SHOW IT TO THE SHERIFF TO GET YOUR REWARD. THEN, GO BACK TO 254.

19.

I HURT MYSELF YESTERDAY. SEPARATED MY SHOULDER. WE WERE IN THE FOREST WHEN WE STUMBLED ONTO A GIGANTIC WEREWOLF. THOSE MONSTROUS BEASTS ARE EXTREMELY DANGEROUS! WE SHOULD ERADICATE THEM...

THE MAN'S WORDS CHILL YOUR BLOOD. IT'S A GOOD THING HE DOESN'T KNOW YOUR SECRET. RETURN ON YOUR STEPS IN 2.

## 20.

I'VE GOT YOU NOW, WHELP!

YOU WERE VERY COURAGEOUS TO ATTACK HIM, BUT SALANDAR CAN ELIMINATE POWERFUL WEREWOLVES, SO A SCARED YOUNG MAN SUCH AS YOURSELF DOESN'T STAND A CHANCE. YOUR ADVENTURE ENDS HERE. TO TRY AGAIN, RETURN TO 1.

## 21.

IF YOU'RE ENTERING THE INFIRMARY FOR THE FIRST TIME, A GHOUL THAT'S GUARDING THE DOOR JUMPS ON YOU AND ATTACKS IN 106.

295

178

319

ON THE OTHER HAND, IF YOU'VE ALREADY BEEN HERE, YOU MAY RUMMAGE AT YOUR LEISURE. TO LEAVE, GO TO 122.

22.
191
269
77

23.
WITH YOUR SHARP SENSES, YOU SMELL THE PIECE OF FABRIC YOU FOUND NEAR THE POOL OF BLOOD. WITHOUT A DOUBT, THAT IS THEDOCRED'S SMELL! GO TO 169.

24.
YOU SHALL NOT PASS!
FRESH WATER HARPY
STRENGTH: 5
HIT POINTS: 17
LOOT: A JADE AMULET AND A POTION THAT GRANTS 2 MAGIC POINTS
XP EARNED: 4
IF YOU WIN THE COMBAT, YOU SEIZE THE JADE AMULET. NOW, YOU JUST NEED TO FIND THE SEER TO GET IT ENCHANTED AND YOU WILL BE ABLE TO TURN INTO A WEREWOLF WHENEVER YOU WANT. MAKE YOUR WAY TO 147.

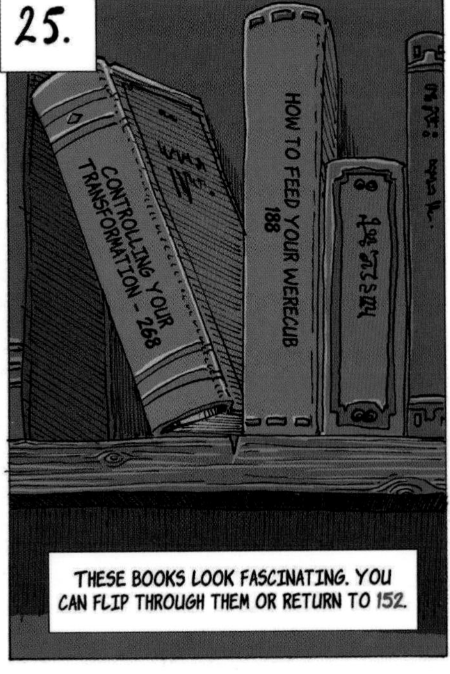
25.
CONTROLLING YOUR TRANSFORMATION - 268
HOW TO FEED YOUR WERECUB 188
THESE BOOKS LOOK FASCINATING. YOU CAN FLIP THROUGH THEM OR RETURN TO 152.

# 26.

97

ALL OF THE EMPLOYEES OF THE MORGUE AND I OFFER YOU OUR SINCEREST CONDOLENCES.

219

TO RETURN TO THE STREET, GO TO 315.

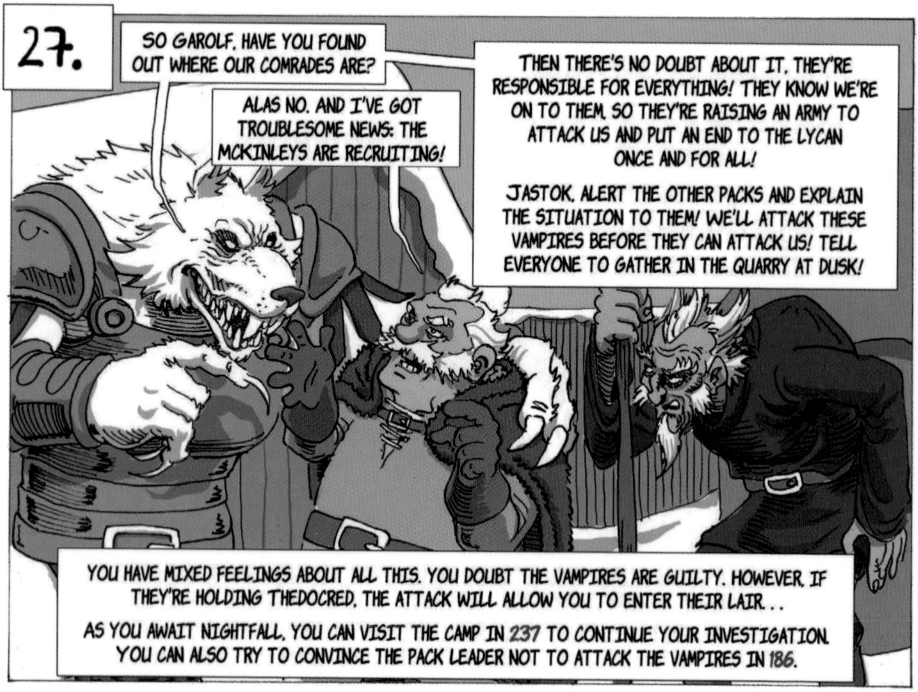

# 27.

SO GAROLF, HAVE YOU FOUND OUT WHERE OUR COMRADES ARE?

ALAS NO. AND I'VE GOT TROUBLESOME NEWS: THE MCKINLEYS ARE RECRUITING!

THEN THERE'S NO DOUBT ABOUT IT, THEY'RE RESPONSIBLE FOR EVERYTHING! THEY KNOW WE'RE ON TO THEM, SO THEY'RE RAISING AN ARMY TO ATTACK US AND PUT AN END TO THE LYCAN ONCE AND FOR ALL!

JASTOK, ALERT THE OTHER PACKS AND EXPLAIN THE SITUATION TO THEM! WE'LL ATTACK THESE VAMPIRES BEFORE THEY CAN ATTACK US! TELL EVERYONE TO GATHER IN THE QUARRY AT DUSK!

YOU HAVE MIXED FEELINGS ABOUT ALL THIS. YOU DOUBT THE VAMPIRES ARE GUILTY. HOWEVER, IF THEY'RE HOLDING THEDOCRED, THE ATTACK WILL ALLOW YOU TO ENTER THEIR LAIR...

AS YOU AWAIT NIGHTFALL, YOU CAN VISIT THE CAMP IN 237 TO CONTINUE YOUR INVESTIGATION. YOU CAN ALSO TRY TO CONVINCE THE PACK LEADER NOT TO ATTACK THE VAMPIRES IN 186.

## 28.

ENTRANCE IS FORBIDDEN, UNLESS YOU CAN GUESS MY PASSWORD: MY FIRST SYLLABLE INTRODUCES CONTRAST, MY SECOND IS TO BE HUMAN, MY THIRD IS A SMALL INSECT. I AM BRIGHTLY COLORED. WHAT AM I?

IF YOU THINK YOU KNOW THE ANSWER, GO TO 40. YOU CAN ALSO ATTACK THE GUARD IN 96 OR DECIDE TO CONTINUE IN THE FOREST IN 63.

## 29.

TROUBLED BY THE CONVERSATION THE LIBRARIAN HAD WITH HER CONTACT, A THOUSAND AND ONE QUESTIONS ARE JOSTLING IN YOUR MIND. BUT TIME IS SHORT AND YOU ONLY HAVE TIME TO ASK TWO OF THEM. CHOOSE CAREFULLY.

- WHY DO ALL THE DEAD PEOPLE COME BACK TO LIFE AS VAMPIRES? 139
- WHERE IS THEDOCRED? 171
- WHO CAPTURED THE WEREWOLVES? 99
- WHAT DOES THE SPIRAL FOUND ON ALL THE DEAD BODIES MEAN? 235

AFTER YOU'VE ASKED YOUR TWO QUESTIONS, GO TO 176.

# 30.

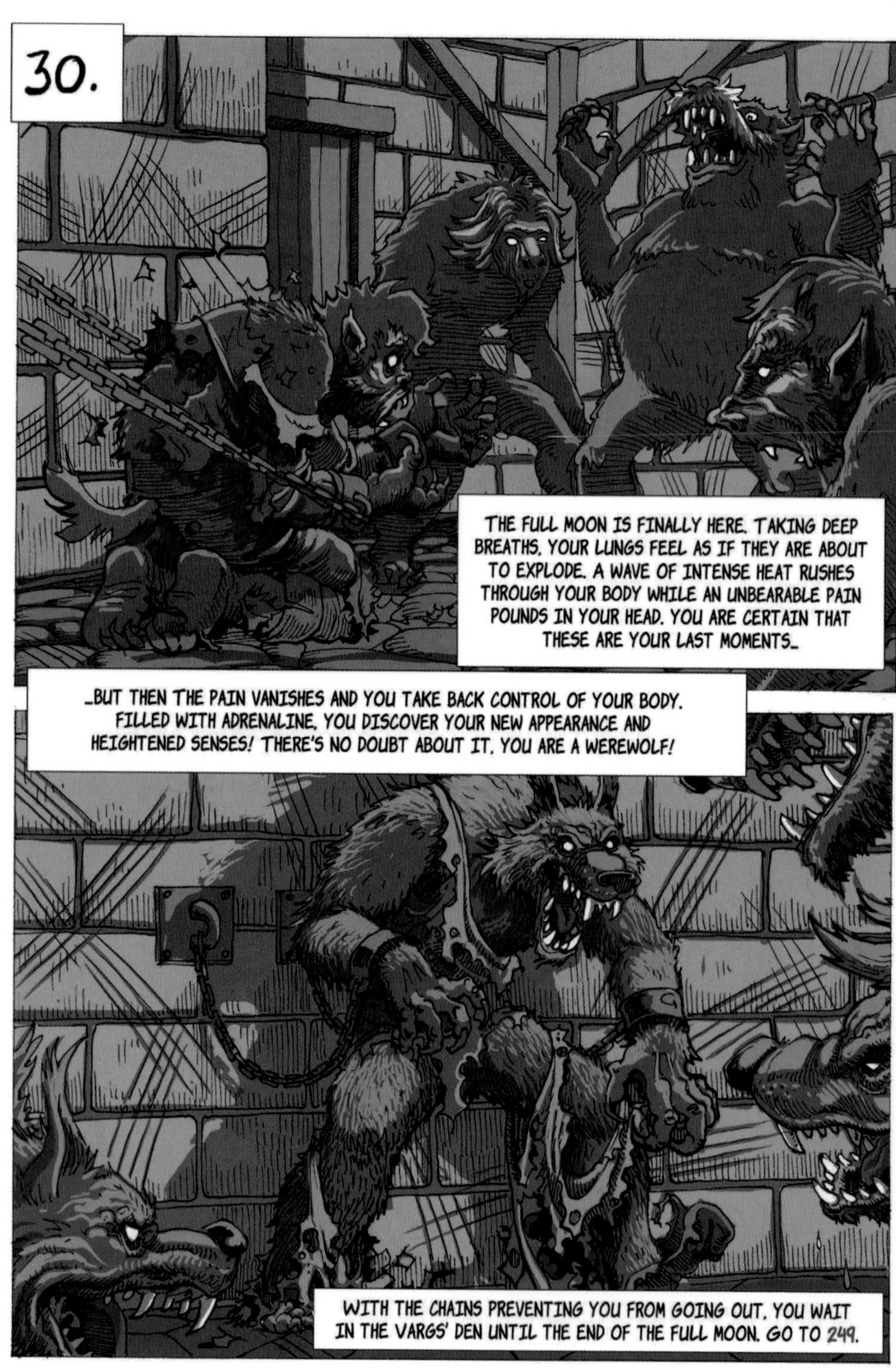
THE FULL MOON IS FINALLY HERE. TAKING DEEP BREATHS, YOUR LUNGS FEEL AS IF THEY ARE ABOUT TO EXPLODE. A WAVE OF INTENSE HEAT RUSHES THROUGH YOUR BODY WHILE AN UNBEARABLE PAIN POUNDS IN YOUR HEAD. YOU ARE CERTAIN THAT THESE ARE YOUR LAST MOMENTS...
...BUT THEN THE PAIN VANISHES AND YOU TAKE BACK CONTROL OF YOUR BODY. FILLED WITH ADRENALINE, YOU DISCOVER YOUR NEW APPEARANCE AND HEIGHTENED SENSES! THERE'S NO DOUBT ABOUT IT, YOU ARE A WEREWOLF!
WITH THE CHAINS PREVENTING YOU FROM GOING OUT, YOU WAIT IN THE VARGS' DEN UNTIL THE END OF THE FULL MOON. GO TO 249.

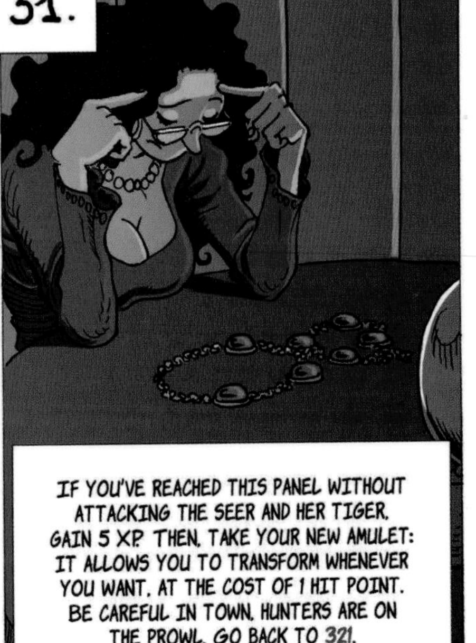
31.
IF YOU'VE REACHED THIS PANEL WITHOUT ATTACKING THE SEER AND HER TIGER, GAIN 5 XP. THEN, TAKE YOUR NEW AMULET: IT ALLOWS YOU TO TRANSFORM WHENEVER YOU WANT, AT THE COST OF 1 HIT POINT. BE CAREFUL IN TOWN, HUNTERS ARE ON THE PROWL. GO BACK TO 321.

32.
181

33.
TROLL
STRENGTH: 14
HIT POINTS: 28
LOOT: 1 POTION THAT GRANTS 3 MAGIC POINTS
XP EARNED: 8
IF YOU WIN THE COMBAT, GO TO 130!

34.
NO VACANCY! GOODBYE!
YOU TAKE A DEEP BREATH IN ORDER TO AVOID YELLING OUT A FEW CHOICE WORDS TO THIS WOMAN! POLITELY AND QUIETLY, HEAD BACK TO 54 TO CONTINUE EXPLORING THE INN.

35.

SHAKING AND AFRAID, THIS VAMPIRE DROPS EVERYTHING AND FLEES! REALIZNG YOU ARE THE SOURCE OF HIS FEAR GIVES YOU AN IDEA. YOU LET OUT A LONG HOWL AND THEN YOU RUN TO 162.

36.

TWO-MOUTHED FROG

STRENGTH: 2
HIT POINTS: 9
LOOT: 5 GP
XP EARNED: 3

IF YOU WIN THE COMBAT, YOU EARN 5 GP AND 3 XP - PROCEED TO 152. IF YOU RUN OUT OF HIT POINTS, YOU ARE DEAD! YOU MUST RESTART YOUR ADVENTURE. GO BACK TO PANEL 1.

## 37.

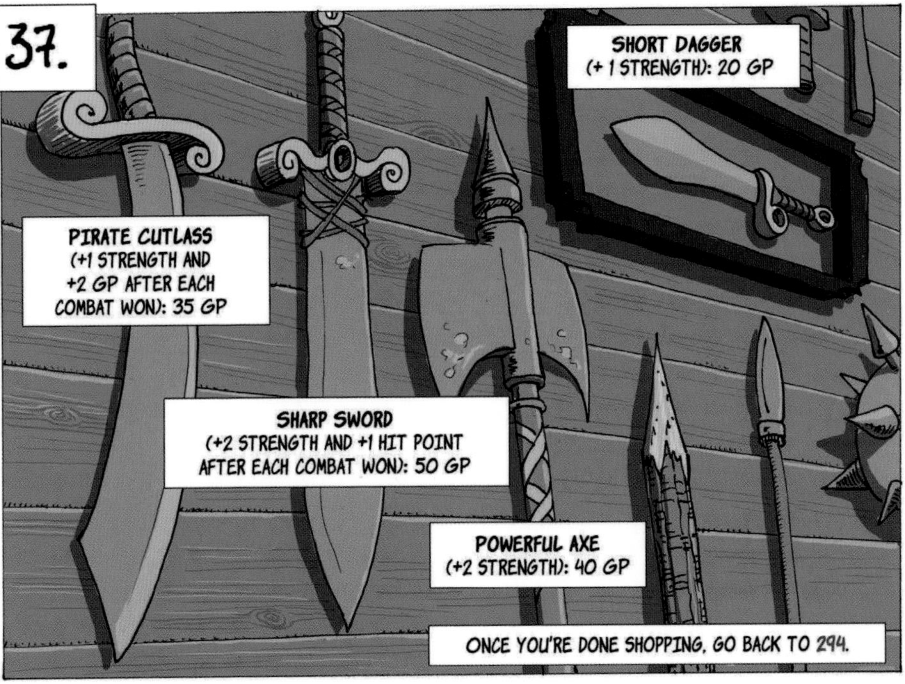

SHORT DAGGER
(+ 1 STRENGTH): 20 GP

PIRATE CUTLASS
(+1 STRENGTH AND
+2 GP AFTER EACH
COMBAT WON): 35 GP

SHARP SWORD
(+2 STRENGTH AND +1 HIT POINT
AFTER EACH COMBAT WON): 50 GP

POWERFUL AXE
(+2 STRENGTH): 40 GP

ONCE YOU'RE DONE SHOPPING, GO BACK TO 294.

## 38.

142
DANGER
223
STOP
KEEP OUT

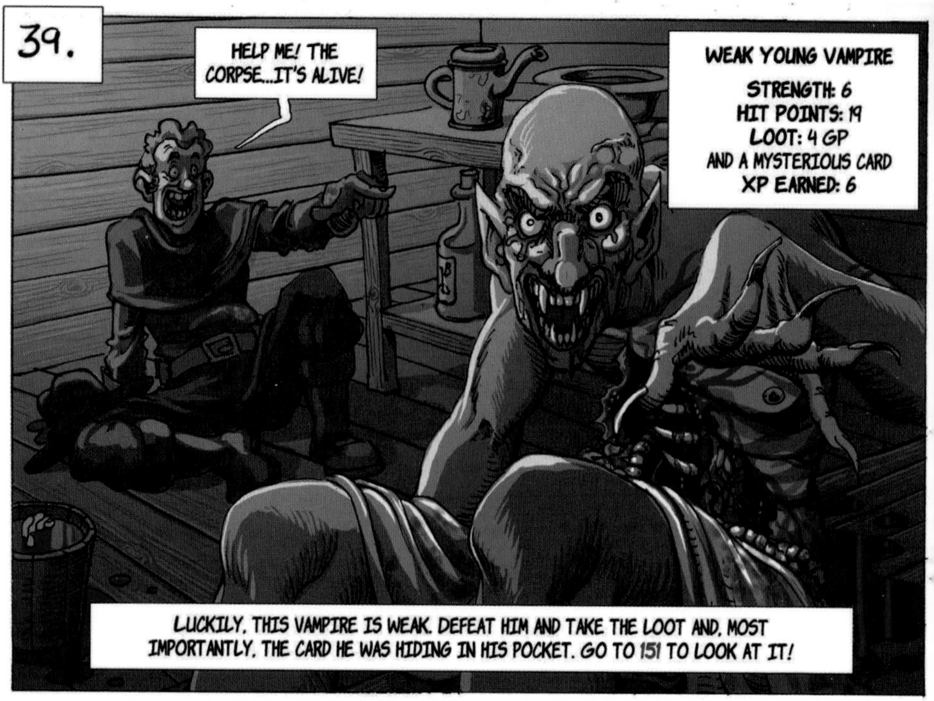

39.

HELP ME! THE CORPSE...IT'S ALIVE!

WEAK YOUNG VAMPIRE
STRENGTH: 6
HIT POINTS: 19
LOOT: 4 GP
AND A MYSTERIOUS CARD
XP EARNED: 6

LUCKILY, THIS VAMPIRE IS WEAK. DEFEAT HIM AND TAKE THE LOOT AND, MOST IMPORTANTLY, THE CARD HE WAS HIDING IN HIS POCKET. GO TO 151 TO LOOK AT IT!

40.
IF YOUR ANSWER IS "BUTTERFLY," CONTINUE TO 276 AND GAIN 4 XP. BUT IF YOU DID NOT FIND THIS ANSWER, YOU MUST EITHER ATTACK THE GUARD IN 96, OR CONTINUE ON YOUR WAY TO 63.

41.
WHO WANTS FRESH MEAT? RIB STEAK FOR ONLY 1 GP!
YOUR WEREWOLF SENSES AWAKEN WHEN YOU NOTICE THE BUTCHER'S STALL. YOUR MOUTH WATERS AS THOSE SMELLS REACH YOUR NOSTRILS...
TO RETURN TO THE MARKETPLACE, GO TO 285.

## 42.

THE PROJECTILES THROWN FROM THE TOP OF THE RAMPARTS MAKE YOU LOSE YOUR BALANCE. GO TO 11 TO SEE WHERE YOU FELL DOWN!

## 43.

IF YOU'RE HERE TO COMPLAIN ABOUT THE WAIT, THERE IS NOTHING I CAN DO! WITH THIS RECENT EPIDEMIC AND THE MURDERS, WE ARE OVERWORKED! WHAT? HMMM LET ME SEE... NO, SORRY. I DO NOT HAVE A THEDOCRED ON MY LIST OF PATIENTS.
TO RETURN TO THE WAITING HALL, GO TO 201.

## 44.

LYCANTHROPY IS A DISEASE CONTRACTED WHEN ONE IS BITTEN OR SCRATCHED BY A WEREWOLF. WHILE SOME LIVE QUITE WELL WITH THIS CURSE, OTHERS DO EVERYTHING THEY CAN TO GET RID OF IT BY EATING CONIWERBERRY. THOSE BERRIES ARE EXTREMELY DIFFICULT TO FIND AND THEIR EFFECTIVENESS REMAINS TO BE SEEN. TAKEN IN HIGH DOSES, THEY COULD EVEN BE DEADLY!

ONCE YOU'RE DONE READING, GO BACK TO 209.

# 45.

DURING COMBAT, YOU ALWAYS GO FIRST! THE FIRST THING TO DO EACH ROUND IS DECIDE WHETHER YOU WILL USE YOUR WEAPON OR MAGIC.
ONCE YOU'VE MADE YOUR CHOICE, LOOK AT YOUR ENEMIES' ATTRIBUTES. HERE, THE TWO-MOUTHED FROG HAS 9 HIT POINTS. TO DEFEAT IT, YOU WILL NEED TO INFLICT AT LEAST 9 POINTS OF DAMAGE DURING COMBAT.
TWO-MOUTHED FROG
STRENGTH: 2
HIT POINTS: 9
LOOT: 5 GP
XP EARNED: 3
2
3
4
5


EACH COMBAT, YOU WILL NEED TO USE THE DISC FOUND IN THE BACK OF THIS BOOK ON PAGE 143 (IF YOU WISH, YOU CAN INSTEAD USE A SIX-SIDED DIE IF YOU HAVE ONE HANDY). HOLD THE DISC TIGHTLY BETWEEN YOUR THUMB AND INDEX FINGER AND SPIN IT. THEN, READ THE RESULT NEXT TO YOUR THUMB. WHEN USING YOUR WEAPON, ADD THE RESULT OF THE SPIN TO YOUR STRENGTH; WHEN USING A SPELL, ADD THE RESULT TO YOUR SPELL'S DAMAGE.

HERE ARE SOME EXAMPLES. I CHOOSE TO FIGHT THIS MONSTER WITH MY MELEE WEAPON. I HAVE A STRENGTH OF 7 AND OBTAIN 2 WITH THE DISC. IN THIS CASE, I INFLICT 9 POINTS OF DAMAGE. I'VE KILLED THE MONSTER WITHOUT TAKING DAMAGE AND EARN THE LOOT AND EXPERIENCE POINTS (XP). IF I HAD OBTAINED 1 WITH THE DISC, THE FROG WOULD STILL BE ALIVE AND IT WOULD GET TO COUNTERATTACK. WITH ITS STRENGTH OF 2, IT INFLICTS 2 POINTS OF DAMAGE (ENEMIES DO NOT SPIN THE DISC). HOWEVER, I GET TO SUBTRACT MY DEFENSE VALUE FROM THE DAMAGE RECEIVED. FOR EXAMPLE, IF I HAVE 1 DEFENSE, I WOULD ONLY LOSE 1 HIT POINT.

THEN, IT IS MY TURN AGAIN. DURING THE PRECEDING ROUND, I INFLICTED 8 POINTS OF DAMAGE. TO KILL IT THIS TURN, I ONLY NEED TO DO 1 MORE DAMAGE. I COULD USE MY WEAPON, LIKE IN THE PREVIOUS ROUND, OR USE A SPELL.

ONCE THE BEAST IS SLAIN, I EARN MY LOOT AND EXPERIENCE!

NOW, LET'S LOOK AT HOW MAGIC SPELLS WORK: WHEN YOU USE A SPELL, YOU DO NOT TAKE YOUR STRENGTH INTO ACCOUNT (STRENGTH IS ONLY USED WITH WEAPONS). YOU ONLY APPLY YOUR SPELL'S CHARACTERISTICS (FOR EXAMPLE, THE SPELL GRANTS 10 POINTS OF DAMAGE). YOU ADD YOUR DISC VALUE TO THIS NUMBER. NOTE THAT SPELLS ARE MORE POWERFUL, BUT YOU MUST SPEND MAGIC POINTS TO USE THEM. YOU BEGIN THE GAME WITH 10 MAGIC POINTS AT THE BEGINNING OF THE GAME, AND YOU MAY EARN MORE DURING YOUR ADVENTURE.

IF YOU'RE READY, BEGIN COMBAT IN PANEL 36! DON'T FORGET TO WRITE DOWN THIS PANEL'S NUMBER IN CASE YOU WISH TO REVIEW THE COMBAT RULES LATER.

## 46.

EXIT
254
108
69

## 47.

YOU SHIVER WHEN YOU SEE THE PEN FILLED WITH ASH HOUNDS. BUT THEY DO GIVE YOU AN IDEA.. MAKE YOUR WAY TO 242 TO FREE THESE MONSTERS!

## 48.

HEY YOU! HELP US WITH THE BATTERING RAM TO GET THAT DOOR OPEN IN 208!

NO! INSTEAD, GIVE US A HAND WITH THE SIEGE TOWER IN 157!

## 49.

THE SEER AND HER TIGER

STRENGTH: 8
HIT POINTS: 25
LOOT: 15 GP
XP EARNED: 2

WE WILL CRUSH YOU, WORM. NO ONE THREATENS US!

IF YOU DEFEAT THEM, BEFORE KILLING THE SEER AND HER TIGER, YOU OFFER HER THEIR LIVES IN EXCHANGE FOR AN ENCHANTED JADE AMULET. IF YOU CHOOSE THIS OPTION, YOU DO NOT TAKE THE LOOT BUT FOLLOW THE SEER IN 31.

ON THE CONTRARY, IF YOU WISH TO END HER DAYS WITHOUT WAITING, TAKE THE LOOT AND GO OUT IN 321. THIS TENT WILL NO LONGER BE AVAILABLE.

50.
SADLY, THIS CHEST IS LOCKED, BUT IF YOU HAVE THE "STREET THIEF" SKILL, YOU OPEN IT AND ACQUIRE A HELMET THAT GRANTS YOU +1 DEFENSE. RETURN TO 322 NOW.

51.
116
70
A MUSTY SMELL ASSAULTS YOUR NOSTRILS IN THIS ROOM. IF YOU CAN'T HANDLE THE SMELL, YOU CAN RETURN TO THE HALLWAY IN 325.

52.
279

53.
165
271

## 54.

306

34

TO RETURN TO THE STREET, GO TO 315.

## 55.

LABORATORY

200

299

## 56.

BUT WHO ARE YOU? HOW DID YOU GET IN? BAH... DOESN'T MATTER. I CAN TELL FROM YOUR SMELL YOU HAVE JUST BEEN TRANSFORMED, HAVEN'T YOU? YOU'VE MANAGED TO EVADE SALANDAR, YOU SAY? NOT BAD. NOT BAD AT ALL YOUNG MAN. HE'S THE BEST TRACKER IN THE BLACK BROTHERHOOD, A WEREWOLF HUNTING CLAN. THEY'RE HARD TO MISS: THEY ALL WEAR A WOLF SKIN ON THEIR BACK AND THEY'VE CHOSEN A HALF-MOON AS THEIR COAT-OF-ARMS.

I AM AT YOUR SERVICE SHOULD YOU WISH TO KNOW MORE ABOUT THE *LOUP GAROU.*

MADAM VARG IS READY TO EXPLAIN A FEW IMPORTANT THINGS ABOUT WEREWOLVES. IF YOU'RE INTERESTED, FOLLOW HER TO 161. OTHERWISE, GO BACK TO 127.

## 57.

IF YOU ANSWERED "SIGNATURE," THE KEY IS YOURS. YOU GAIN 6 XP AND MAY GO BACK TO 21! IF YOU DID NOT GET THE CORRECT ANSWER, YOU WILL NEED TO FIGHT FOR THIS KEY! GO TO 193.

58.
MY FATHER IS IN TOWN AND IS LOOKING FOR CLUES TO FIND THEM. WE'VE LEARNED THAT YOUR MASTER HAS ALSO DISAPPEARED! MAYBE WE'RE DEALING WITH THE SAME KIDNAPPERS.
TO RETURN TO THE MAIN ROOM, GO TO 167.

59.
LIKE A RAT IN A TRAP, SALANDAR'S CAUGHT YOU NOW! RESTART THE ADVENTURE IN 1!

60.

231

286

92

265

NO MATTER HOW HARD YOU CALL FOR YOUR MASTER, NOBODY ANSWERS. THE BLOOD STAINS ON THE FLOOR ONLY CONFIRM YOUR SUSPICIONS. SOMETHING HAS HAPPENED TO HIM.

# 61.

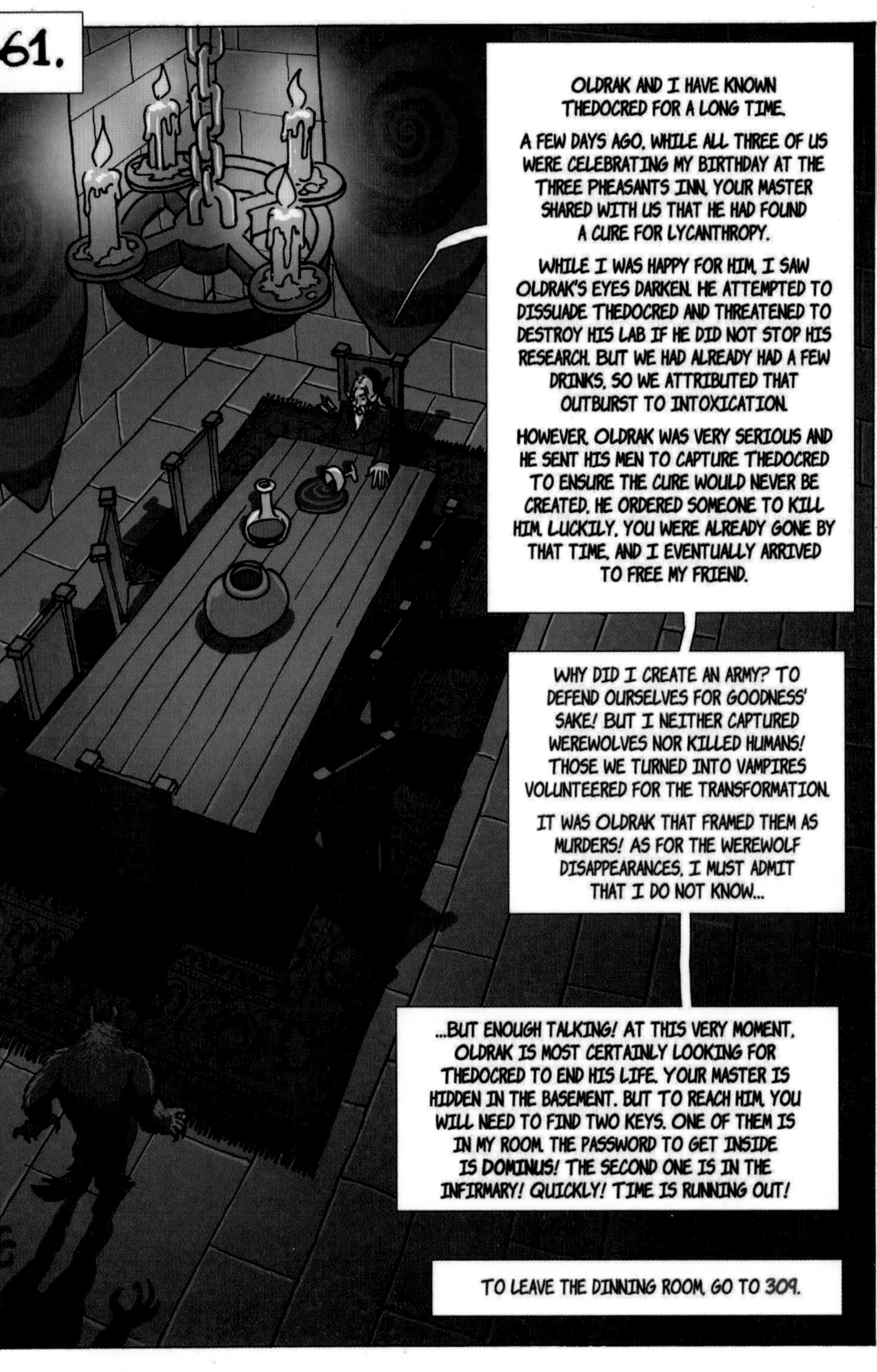
OLDRAK AND I HAVE KNOWN THEDOCRED FOR A LONG TIME.
A FEW DAYS AGO, WHILE ALL THREE OF US WERE CELEBRATING MY BIRTHDAY AT THE THREE PHEASANTS INN, YOUR MASTER SHARED WITH US THAT HE HAD FOUND A CURE FOR LYCANTHROPY.
WHILE I WAS HAPPY FOR HIM, I SAW OLDRAK'S EYES DARKEN. HE ATTEMPTED TO DISSUADE THEDOCRED AND THREATENED TO DESTROY HIS LAB IF HE DID NOT STOP HIS RESEARCH. BUT WE HAD ALREADY HAD A FEW DRINKS, SO WE ATTRIBUTED THAT OUTBURST TO INTOXICATION.
HOWEVER, OLDRAK WAS VERY SERIOUS AND HE SENT HIS MEN TO CAPTURE THEDOCRED TO ENSURE THE CURE WOULD NEVER BE CREATED. HE ORDERED SOMEONE TO KILL HIM. LUCKILY, YOU WERE ALREADY GONE BY THAT TIME, AND I EVENTUALLY ARRIVED TO FREE MY FRIEND.
WHY DID I CREATE AN ARMY? TO DEFEND OURSELVES FOR GOODNESS' SAKE! BUT I NEITHER CAPTURED WEREWOLVES NOR KILLED HUMANS! THOSE WE TURNED INTO VAMPIRES VOLUNTEERED FOR THE TRANSFORMATION.
IT WAS OLDRAK THAT FRAMED THEM AS MURDERS! AS FOR THE WEREWOLF DISAPPEARANCES, I MUST ADMIT THAT I DO NOT KNOW...
...BUT ENOUGH TALKING! AT THIS VERY MOMENT, OLDRAK IS MOST CERTAINLY LOOKING FOR THEDOCRED TO END HIS LIFE. YOUR MASTER IS HIDDEN IN THE BASEMENT. BUT TO REACH HIM, YOU WILL NEED TO FIND TWO KEYS. ONE OF THEM IS IN MY ROOM. THE PASSWORD TO GET INSIDE IS DOMINUS! THE SECOND ONE IS IN THE INFIRMARY! QUICKLY! TIME IS RUNNING OUT!
TO LEAVE THE DINNING ROOM, GO TO 309.

## 62.

SHERIFF

220

MORGUE

241

IF YOU ARE IN WEREWOLF FORM, YOU FEEL A BLADE AGAINST YOUR THROAT. GO TO 192.

IF YOU ARE IN HUMAN FORM, YOU MAY GO TO THE SHERIFF'S OR THE MORGUE. TO RETURN TO THE TOWN MAP, GO TO 180.

## 63.

AND TO THINK THAT THE SEER PREDICTED A MILD WINTER. IF IT DOESN'T STOP SNOWING, WE'RE GONNA FREEZE IN OUR TRACKS! ALL RIGHTY THEN, I'VE GOTTA GO AND BRING THIS WOOD BACK TO WARM MY HOUSE. DON'T BE A STRANGER! IT'S THE HOUSE WITH THE BLUE DOOR THAT'S GOT MY NAME ON IT: VINUS.

YOU WAVE TO THE NICE MAN AS YOU HEAD BACK ON THE ROAD IN 13.

64.

65.
OY. IT'S A GOOD THING THAT ROBBER DID NOT FOLLOW YOU! YOU CAN CONTINUE ON YOUR WAY IN 293, KNOWING HE WILL ATTACK THAT POOR WOMAN INSTEAD OF YOU. BUT, IF YOU'RE HAVING REGRETS, YOU CAN RETURN TO FIGHT HIM IN 175!

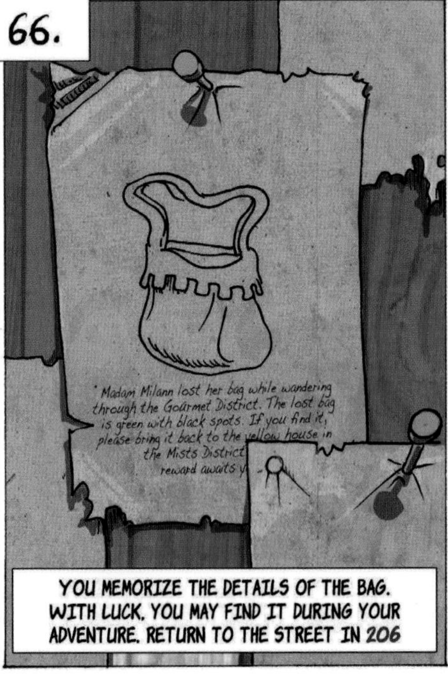
66.
Madam Milann lost her bag while wandering through the Gourmet District. The lost bag is green with black spots. If you find it, please bring it back to the yellow house in the Mists District
reward awaits y
YOU MEMORIZE THE DETAILS OF THE BAG. WITH LUCK, YOU MAY FIND IT DURING YOUR ADVENTURE. RETURN TO THE STREET IN 206

67.

THE STONES COMING FROM ABOVE WERE NOT ENOUGH TO KEEP YOU FROM REACHING THE TOP OF THE RAMPARTS! NOW, YOU MUST FIND WHERE YOUR MASTER IS HIDING! GO TO 89!

68.

309

122

279

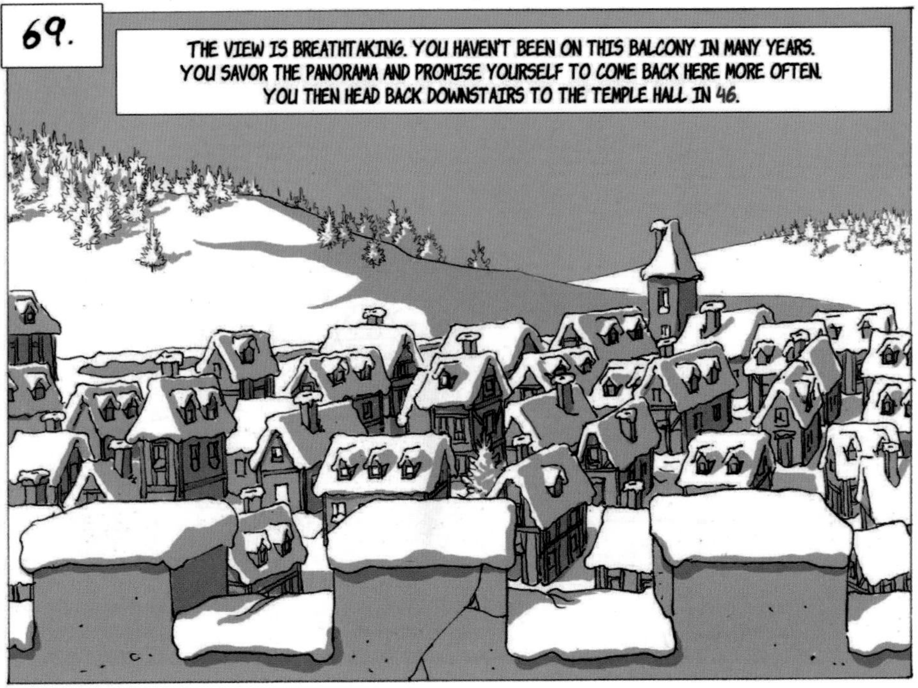

69.

THE VIEW IS BREATHTAKING. YOU HAVEN'T BEEN ON THIS BALCONY IN MANY YEARS. YOU SAVOR THE PANORAMA AND PROMISE YOURSELF TO COME BACK HERE MORE OFTEN. YOU THEN HEAD BACK DOWNSTAIRS TO THE TEMPLE HALL IN 46.

70.

THAT'S SALANDAR, THE FAMOUS WEREWOLF HUNTER! HE COMES FROM THE KINGDOM OF CNAKOVY. RUMOR HAS IT THAT HE DRINKS FROST VENIN EACH MORNING TO GET STRONGER. ME, I'M NOT SCARED OF HIM!
AFTER YOUR CONVERSATION, GO BACK TO 51!

71.

ONCE YOU'VE PUT ON THE KNOCKED OUT EMPLOYEE'S UNIFORM, YOU CAN GO BACK TO THE BLADES DISTRICT SQUARE IN 62.

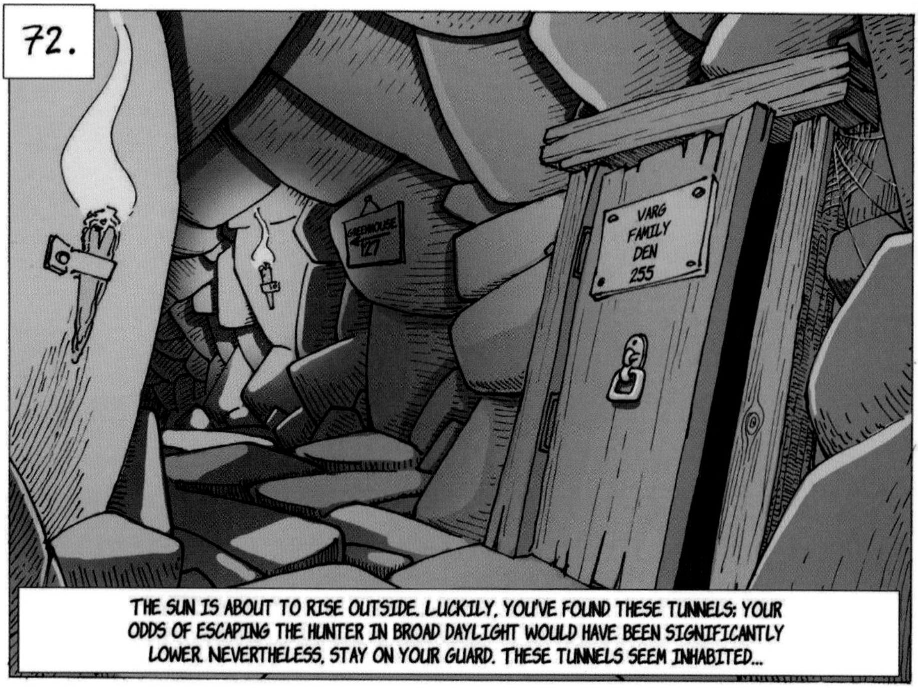

## 72.

GREENHOUSE
127

VARG
FAMILY
DEN
255

THE SUN IS ABOUT TO RISE OUTSIDE. LUCKILY, YOU'VE FOUND THESE TUNNELS; YOUR ODDS OF ESCAPING THE HUNTER IN BROAD DAYLIGHT WOULD HAVE BEEN SIGNIFICANTLY LOWER. NEVERTHELESS, STAY ON YOUR GUARD. THESE TUNNELS SEEM INHABITED...

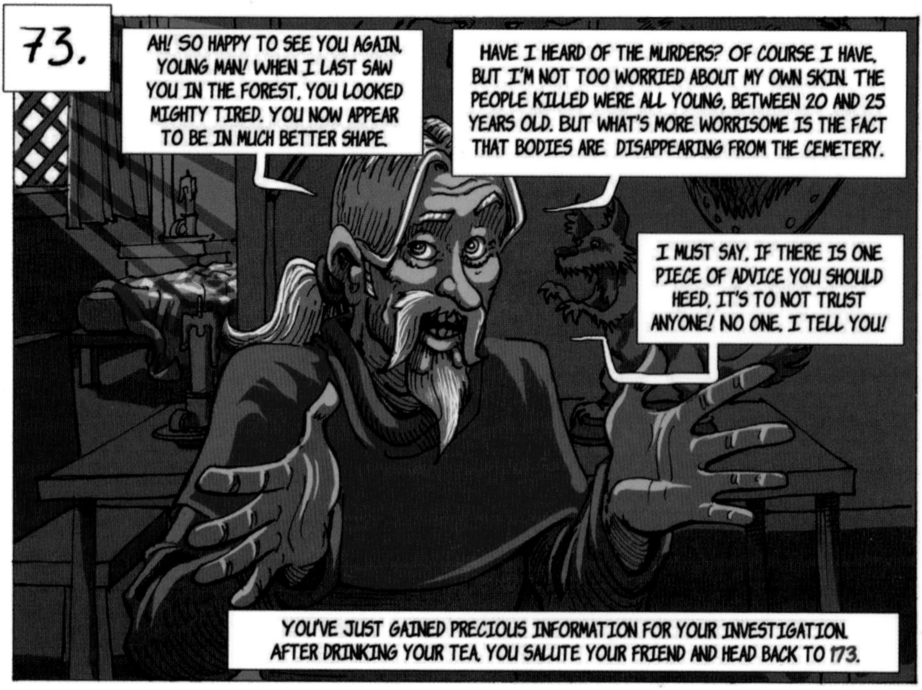

## 73.

AH! SO HAPPY TO SEE YOU AGAIN, YOUNG MAN! WHEN I LAST SAW YOU IN THE FOREST, YOU LOOKED MIGHTY TIRED. YOU NOW APPEAR TO BE IN MUCH BETTER SHAPE.

HAVE I HEARD OF THE MURDERS? OF COURSE I HAVE, BUT I'M NOT TOO WORRIED ABOUT MY OWN SKIN. THE PEOPLE KILLED WERE ALL YOUNG, BETWEEN 20 AND 25 YEARS OLD. BUT WHAT'S MORE WORRISOME IS THE FACT THAT BODIES ARE DISAPPEARING FROM THE CEMETERY.

I MUST SAY, IF THERE IS ONE PIECE OF ADVICE YOU SHOULD HEED, IT'S TO NOT TRUST ANYONE! NO ONE, I TELL YOU!

YOU'VE JUST GAINED PRECIOUS INFORMATION FOR YOUR INVESTIGATION. AFTER DRINKING YOUR TEA, YOU SALUTE YOUR FRIEND AND HEAD BACK TO 173.

74.

BROTHERS, IT IS TIME! WE WILL FINALLY OUST OUR OLD ENEMY FROM THIS FORTRESS AND FREE OUR OWN! NO MERCY FOR THOSE BLOOD SUCKERS. I WANT THEM ALL DEAD!
CHARGE!
YOU HOWL IN THE NIGHT WITH THE WOLVES AT YOUR SIDE. YOUR HOWLS FILL THE AIR AND YOU POUNCE INTO THE BATTLE HOPING TO GET INSIDE THE FORTRESS IN TIME TO FIND YOUR MASTER. GO TO 304.

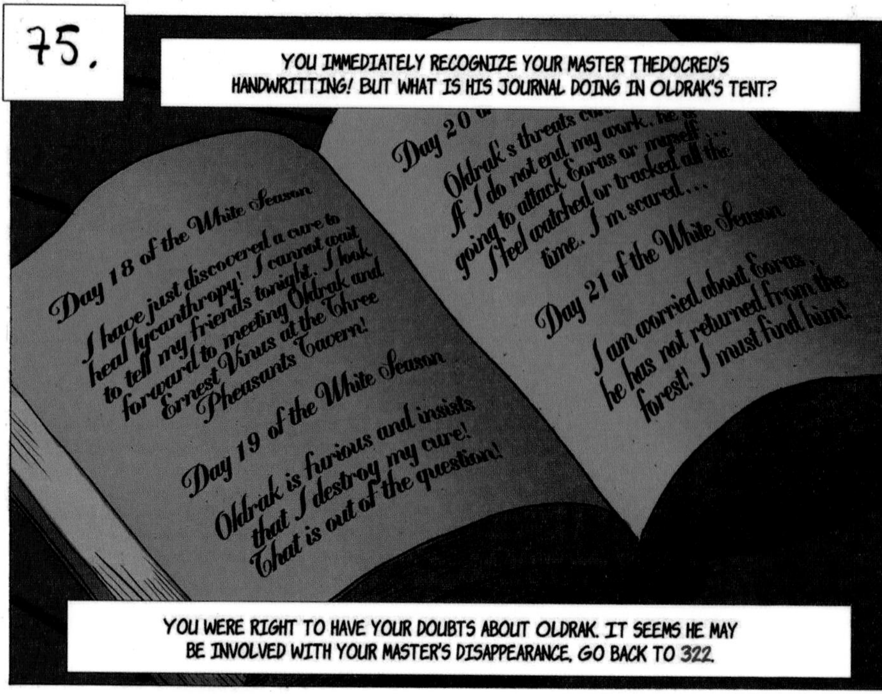

75.

YOU IMMEDIATELY RECOGNIZE YOUR MASTER THEDOCRED'S HANDWRITTING! BUT WHAT IS HIS JOURNAL DOING IN OLDRAK'S TENT?

Day 18 of the White Season

I have just discovered a cure to heal lycanthropy! I cannot wait to tell my friends tonight. I look forward to meeting Oldrak and Ernest Vinus at the Three Pheasants Tavern!

Day 19 of the White Season

Oldrak is furious and insists that I destroy my cure! That is out of the question!

Day 20 ...

Oldrak's threats ... If I do not end my work, he is going to attack Eoras or myself... I feel watched or tracked all the time. I'm scared...

Day 21 of the White Season

I am worried about Eoras, he has not returned from the forest! I must find him!

YOU WERE RIGHT TO HAVE YOUR DOUBTS ABOUT OLDRAK. IT SEEMS HE MAY BE INVOLVED WITH YOUR MASTER'S DISAPPEARANCE. GO BACK TO 322.

76.
AS YOU'RE READING ONE OF THE SCROLLS ALOUD, A WORRISOME SMOKE STARTS SPREADING AROUND YOU. IT ENTERS YOUR NOSE AND MOUTH AND CONTINUES ITS WAY INSIDE YOU. SHAKEN, YOU QUICKLY MOVE AWAY FROM THE CHEST TO 276. THIS TENT IS NO LONGER ACCESSIBLE. YOU LOSE 2 HIT POINTS, BUT GAIN 5 GP.

77.
204
22

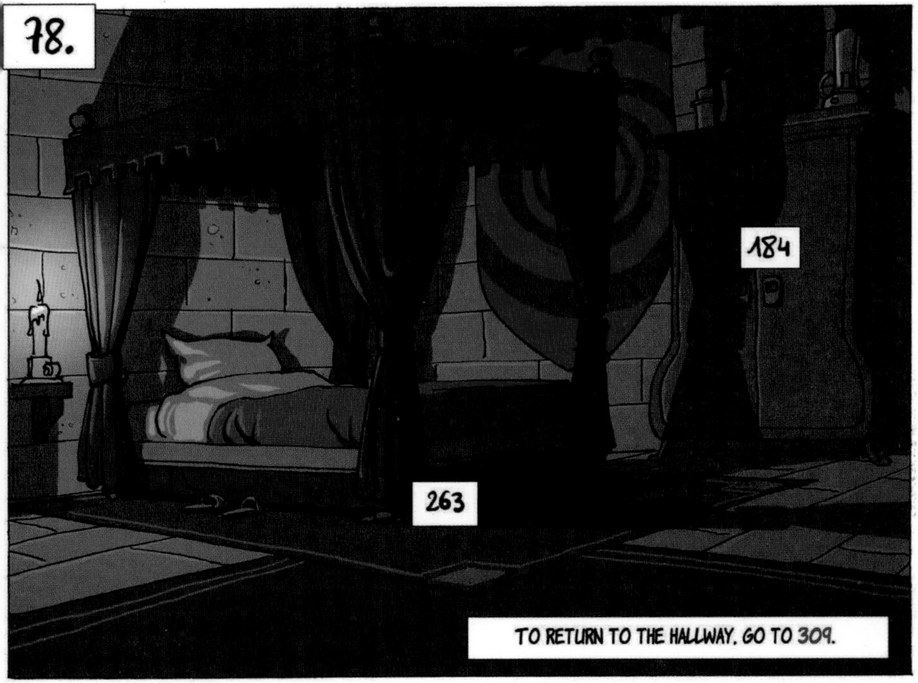

78.

184

263

TO RETURN TO THE HALLWAY, GO TO 309.

79.

THE PEOPLE THAT HAVE COME HERE ARE SICK BECAUSE OF THE BAD WEATHER. BUT FOR THE LAST TWO DAYS, MANY PEOPLE HAVE BEEN FOUND DEAD, AND THEY DID NOT DIE BECAUSE OF THE COLD! ALL OF THEM HAD BEEN DRAINED OF THEIR BLOOD. HOW AWFUL! NO WONDER THE TOWNSFOLK ARE HIDING AND BARRICADING THEIR HOMES AT NIGHTFALL. THE NEXT VICTIM COULD BE ANYONE.

THE MONK DOES NOT HAVE ANY MORE TIME FOR YOU. RETURN TO 297.

80.
OOPS! BY STEPPING ON THAT TWIG, YOU'VE ATTRACTED THE HUNTER'S ATTENTION. HE TURNS AROUND AND SEES YOU! THE CHASE CONTINUES IN 211.

## 81.

THE WEAPONS ARE CHAINED TO THE WALL. YOU ARE UNABLE TO TAKE ANYTHING, EXCEPT FOR THIS LOOSELY CHAINED SHIELD THAT GRANTS +2 DEFENSE, SHOULD YOU CHOOSE TO WIELD IT!

RETURN TO THE HALLWAY IN 143.

## 82.

TO RETURN TO THE MOAT DISTRICT, GO TO 321.

83.

THE PASSWORD IS "BLACK WIDOW!" PLEASE LET ME GO NOW? I PROMISE I WON'T TELL ANYONE.

YOU MAKE NOTE OF THIS PRECIOUS CODE WORD AND HEAD BACK TO THE BLADES DISTRICT SQUARE IN 62.

84.
238
THIS IS WHERE MY FAMILY AND I TRANSFORM ON FULL MOON NIGHTS. IT IS SMALL, BUT HERE, NO ONE CAN FIND OR HEAR US.

85.
LOOKING FOR A NEW WEAPON? GO TO 37!
TO RETURN TO THE STREET, GO TO 294.

86.

YOU LOOK CLOSER AT ONE OF THE COINS AND NOTICE THAT THEY WERE ALL STRUCK WITH A HALF-MOON, THE INSIGNIA OF THE BLACK BROTHERHOOD. GO BACK TO 166.

87.

199


88.

ALL YOUR TRAINING IS PAYING OFF. YOUR AGILITY ALLOWS YOU TO CARTWHEEL, GRAB A SHIELD, AND GET TO SAFETY. SADLY, THE SIEGE TOWER IS NOW TOO FAR FOR YOU TO REACH IT. TO MAKE MATTERS WORSE, A HORDE OF VAMPIRES AND TROLLS IS CLOSING IN ON YOU IN 103.

89.

143

279

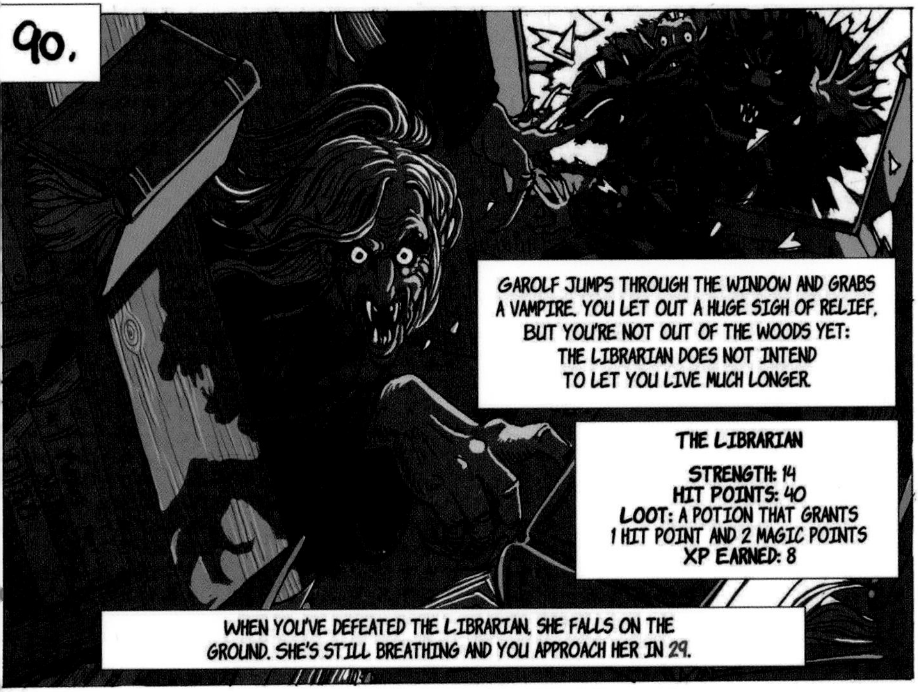

90.

GAROLF JUMPS THROUGH THE WINDOW AND GRABS A VAMPIRE. YOU LET OUT A HUGE SIGH OF RELIEF. BUT YOU'RE NOT OUT OF THE WOODS YET: THE LIBRARIAN DOES NOT INTEND TO LET YOU LIVE MUCH LONGER.

THE LIBRARIAN

STRENGTH: 14
HIT POINTS: 40
LOOT: A POTION THAT GRANTS 1 HIT POINT AND 2 MAGIC POINTS
XP EARNED: 8

WHEN YOU'VE DEFEATED THE LIBRARIAN, SHE FALLS ON THE GROUND. SHE'S STILL BREATHING AND YOU APPROACH HER IN 29.

91.
110
211
SALANDAR IS STILL CHASING YOU! YOU CAN FACE HIM IN 20, OR KEEP RUNNING AWAY BY CHOOSING ONE OF THE PATHS.

92.
THIS CHEST SEEMS LOCKED. YOU CAN OPEN IT ONLY IF YOU HAVE THE "STREET THIEF" SKILL. IF YOU DO, TAKE THE 15 GP THAT ARE INSIDE. GO BACK TO 60.

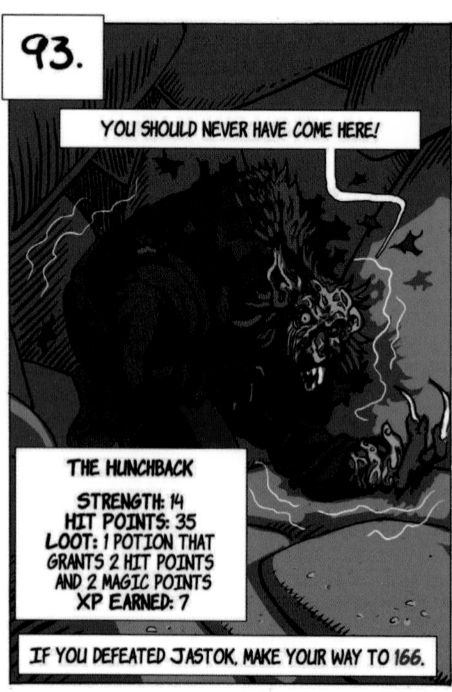
93.
YOU SHOULD NEVER HAVE COME HERE!
THE HUNCHBACK
STRENGTH: 14
HIT POINTS: 35
LOOT: 1 POTION THAT GRANTS 2 HIT POINTS AND 2 MAGIC POINTS
XP EARNED: 7
IF YOU DEFEATED JASTOK, MAKE YOUR WAY TO 166.

94.
VAMPIRE
STRENGTH: 15
HIT POINTS: 20
LOOT: A STRONG AX (+2 STRENGTH)
XP EARNED: 4
CONTINUE IN 135.

95.

WELCOME, SOLDIER. LET ME HEAL YOUR WOUNDS BEFORE THE GREAT BATTLE!

WHEN THE HEALER PUTS HER HANDS ON YOUR TORSO, YOU FEEL A GREAT WARMTH COURSE THROUGH YOUR BODY. YOU GAIN 2 HIT POINTS. RETURN TO 237. THIS PANEL IS NO LONGER AVAILABLE.

96.

RATHER DARING TO TAKE ON A SOLDIER! FIRMLY HELD TO THE GROUND, EVEN WITH YOUR NEW POWERS, YOU CANNOT GET BACK UP! YOUR ADVENTURE ENDS HERE, UNLESS YOU PAY A 15 GP FINE. IF YOU CHOOSE THIS OPTION, YOU MAY NO LONGER ENTER THE CAMP. CONTINUE ON YOUR WAY IN 63.

97.

IF I EVER FIND THE PERSON THAT'S BEEN GRAVE ROBBING AT NIGHT, HE'LL EAT MY SHOVEL, I TELL YA! I HAVE BETTER THINGS TO DO THAN DIGGING THESE TOMBS OVER AND OVER AGAIN. NOW LEAVE ME ALONE, I HAVE WORK TO DO!

YOU WON'T GET ANYTHING ELSE FROM HIM. RETURN TO THE CEMETERY ENTRANCE IN 26.

98.
IF YOUR ANSWER IS "BAR," THE TOMBSTONE OPENS AND REVEALS A STAIRCASE THAT TAKES YOU TO 144. YOU GAIN 2 XP FOR SOLVING THE RIDDLE. IF YOU HADN'T FOUND THE ANSWER, GO BACK TO 64. THIS PANEL IS NO LONGER AVAILABLE.

99.
IT IS NOT US! ALAS, I CANNOT TELL YOU MORE. I DO NOT KNOW THE ANSWER TO YOUR QUESTION... BEUARGL!!!
IF YOU HAVE A SECOND QUESTION, RETURN TO 29, OTHERWISE GO TO 176.

# 100.

CHAIN MAIL TUNIC: (+ 2 DEFENSE): 40 GP
PAIR OF GLOVES: (+ 1 DEFENSE): 20 GP
PAIR OF BOOTS: (+ 1 DEFENSE): 20 GP
HELM: (+ 1 DEFENSE): 20 GP
SHIELD: (+ 3 DEFENSE): 60 GP

TO RETURN TO THE MARKET PLACE, GO TO 285.

# 101.

NICE SHOT KID! WE DID IT!

YOUR HEART IS RACING AS THE ENEMY CATAPULT EXPLODES INTO SPLINTERS.
YOU RAISE YOUR WEAPON AND SHIELD AND HEAD TO THE RAMPARTS IN 135!

## 102.

EORAS, HERE IS WHAT I'M PROPOSING. IF YOU HOPE TO KNOW MORE ABOUT THEDOCRED AND THOSE VAMPIRES, FOLLOW ME TO MY PACK'S CAMP. IT IS SEVERAL MILES FROM WHITEHORN, HIDDEN NEAR THE OLD WHITE OAK. THERE, WE'LL BE ABLE TO CONTINUE OUR INVESTIGATION TOGETHER! WHAT SAY YOU?

IF YOU HAVE NOTHING ELSE TO DO IN TOWN, FOLLOW GAROLF TO 301. ON THE OTHER HAND, IF YOU ARE NOT DONE EXPLORING WHITETHORN, YOU CAN GO BACK TO IT BY LOOKING AT YOUR MAP IN 180. WHEN YOU ARE DONE, JOIN GAROLF IN 301. WRITE THIS NUMBER ON YOUR CHARACTER SHEET AS A REMINDER.

## 103.

**FIRE BAT**

**BONUS:** AT THE END OF EACH COMBAT ROUND, GAIN 1 MAGIC POINT.

**MOUNTAIN TROLL**

**STRENGTH:** 16
**HIT POINTS:** 25
**LOOT:** A POTION THAT GRANTS 2 MAGIC POINTS
**XP EARNED:** 7

AFTER VANQUISHING THE TROLL, CHOOSE THE LEFT VAMPIRE IN 290 OR THE RIGHT ONE IN 94. IF YOU HAVE THE "ANIMAL HUSBANDRY" SKILL, THE FIRE BAT FLIES TO YOUR SIDE. NOTE THAT IF YOU ALREADY HAVE A COMPANION, YOU MUST CHOOSE ONE TO KEEP!

## 104.

TO OUR LEFT IS OLDRAK'S TENT!

TO SPEAK TO THE YOUNG LADY WHO'S SHARPENING HER SWORD, GO TO 281. TO TAKE A LOOK IN THE PACK LEADER'S TENT, TURN TO 168. TO RETURN TO THE CAMP ENTRANCE, MAKE YOUR WAY TO 237.

YOU MAY ALSO GO DIRECTLY TO THE QUARRY IN 277, BUT NOTE THAT IF YOU DO SO, YOU WILL NO LONGER BE ABLE TO RETURN TO THE CAMP!

## 105.

NOTHING REALLY INTERESTING AROUND HERE, OTHER THAN THESE 3 FOOD BUCKETS. EACH OF THEM GRANTS 1 HIT POINT. YOU CAN STEAL SOME, BUT IT IS THIEVERY. BE CAREFUL, SUCH ACTIONS HAVE CONSEQUENCES. GO BACK TO 209!

## 106.

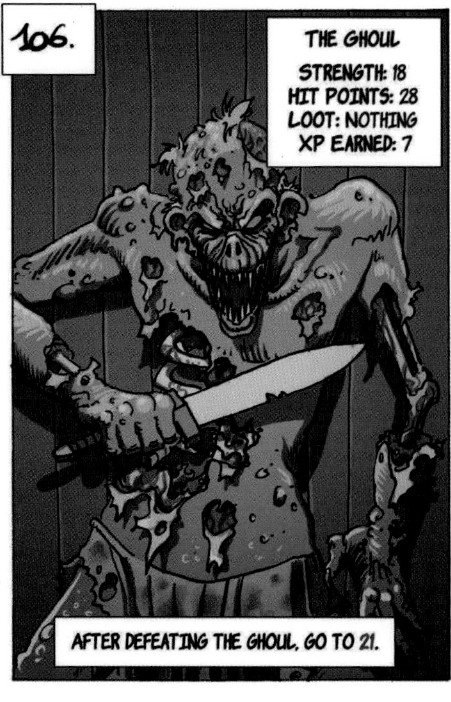
THE GHOUL
STRENGTH: 18
HIT POINTS: 28
LOOT: NOTHING
XP EARNED: 7
AFTER DEFEATING THE GHOUL, GO TO 21.

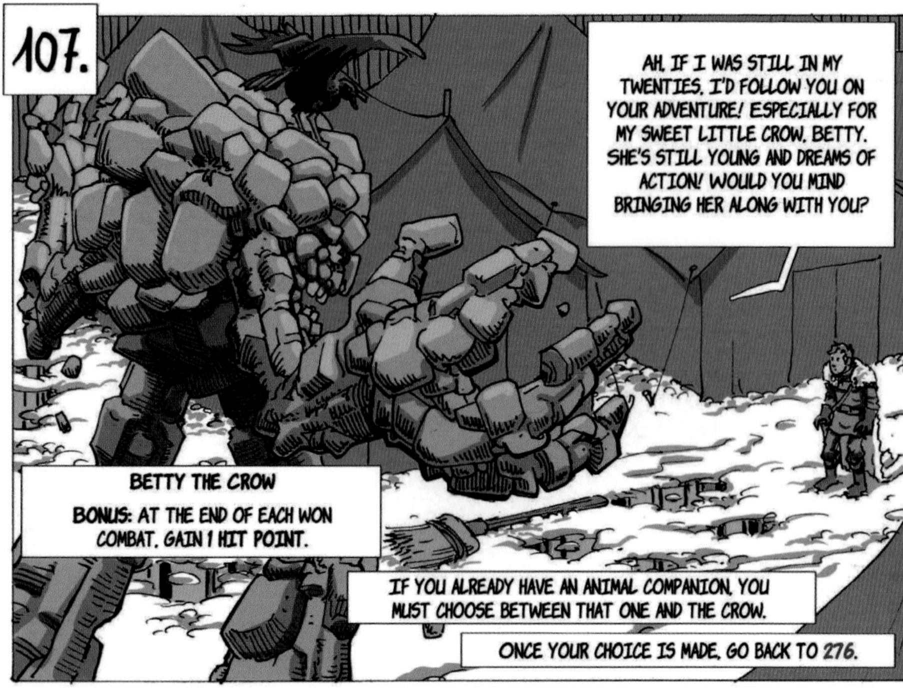

107.

AH, IF I WAS STILL IN MY TWENTIES, I'D FOLLOW YOU ON YOUR ADVENTURE! ESPECIALLY FOR MY SWEET LITTLE CROW, BETTY. SHE'S STILL YOUNG AND DREAMS OF ACTION! WOULD YOU MIND BRINGING HER ALONG WITH YOU?

BETTY THE CROW

BONUS: AT THE END OF EACH WON COMBAT, GAIN 1 HIT POINT.

IF YOU ALREADY HAVE AN ANIMAL COMPANION, YOU MUST CHOOSE BETWEEN THAT ONE AND THE CROW.

ONCE YOUR CHOICE IS MADE, GO BACK TO 276.

108.
HELLO EORAS. WHAT BRINGS YOU HERE TODAY?
IF YOU WISH TO INQUIRE ABOUT THE DEAD, GO TO 283. YOU MAY ALSO PRAY IN 189, OR GO BACK TO THE TEMPLE HALL IN 46.

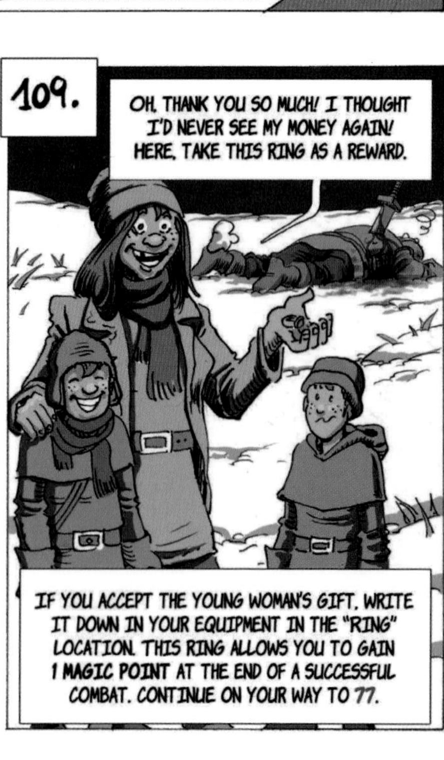
109.
OH, THANK YOU SO MUCH! I THOUGHT I'D NEVER SEE MY MONEY AGAIN! HERE, TAKE THIS RING AS A REWARD.
IF YOU ACCEPT THE YOUNG WOMAN'S GIFT, WRITE IT DOWN IN YOUR EQUIPMENT IN THE "RING" LOCATION. THIS RING ALLOWS YOU TO GAIN 1 MAGIC POINT AT THE END OF A SUCCESSFUL COMBAT. CONTINUE ON YOUR WAY TO 77.

110.
289

111.
THAT NECKLACE BELONGED TO THE LEADER OF THE ASSASSIN'S GUILD! GREAT WORK! HERE, TAKE THESE 20 GP FOR YOUR TROUBLE!
ONCE YOU'VE POCKETED YOUR REWARD, GO BACK TO 220.

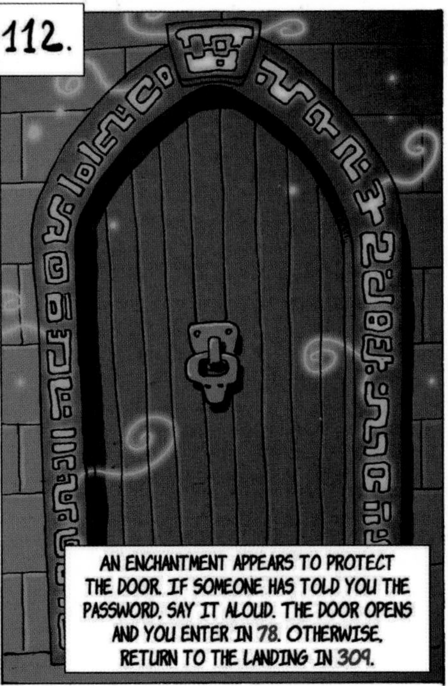
112.
AN ENCHANTMENT APPEARS TO PROTECT THE DOOR. IF SOMEONE HAS TOLD YOU THE PASSWORD, SAY IT ALOUD. THE DOOR OPENS AND YOU ENTER IN 78. OTHERWISE, RETURN TO THE LANDING IN 309.

113.
IT WOULD SEEM THAT THEDOCRED WAS PACKING HIS BAG BEFORE HE WAS ATTACKED.
GO TO 231.

114.
IF YOU HAVE IN YOUR POSSESSION THE BAG OF DARKNESS, GO TO 212! IF YOU DO NOT HAVE IT, BUT WISH TO DISCUSS WITH THE GIANT, GO TO 107. IF YOU PREFER TO IGNORE THE CREATURE, GO BACK TO 276. YOU MAY NOT RETURN HERE AGAIN.

115.
FOR 10 GP, I'LL SHARPEN YOUR BLADE. THIS'LL GRANT IT +1 STRENGTH.
RETURN TO 281.

116.

HOW DID YOU GET IN? OH, YOU FOUND MY KEY! I THOUGHT I'D NEVER SEE IT AGAIN! I LOST IT THE OTHER NIGHT WHILE COMING HOME! HERE, TO SHOW YOU MY GRATITUDE, TAKE ONE OF THESE ITEMS!

SHIELD
(+1 DEFENSE)

KNIFE
(+1 STRENGTH)

AFTER MAKING YOUR CHOICE, GO BACK TO 51!

117.
THE PROJECTILE THAT JUST HIT YOU SHATTERED THE BATTERING RAM TO BITS. HURT, YOU LOSE 1 HIT POINT AND STAGGER BACK TO YOUR FEET. YOU CAN RETURN TO THE BATTLE IN 103, OR HEAD TOWARDS A SIEGE ENGINE IN 149.

118.

119.

YOU SPOT TWO VAMPIRES BEHIND THE SHELVES DISCUSSING SOMETHING. YOU APPROACH DISCREETLY TO LISTEN IN ON THEIR CONVERSATION IN 150.

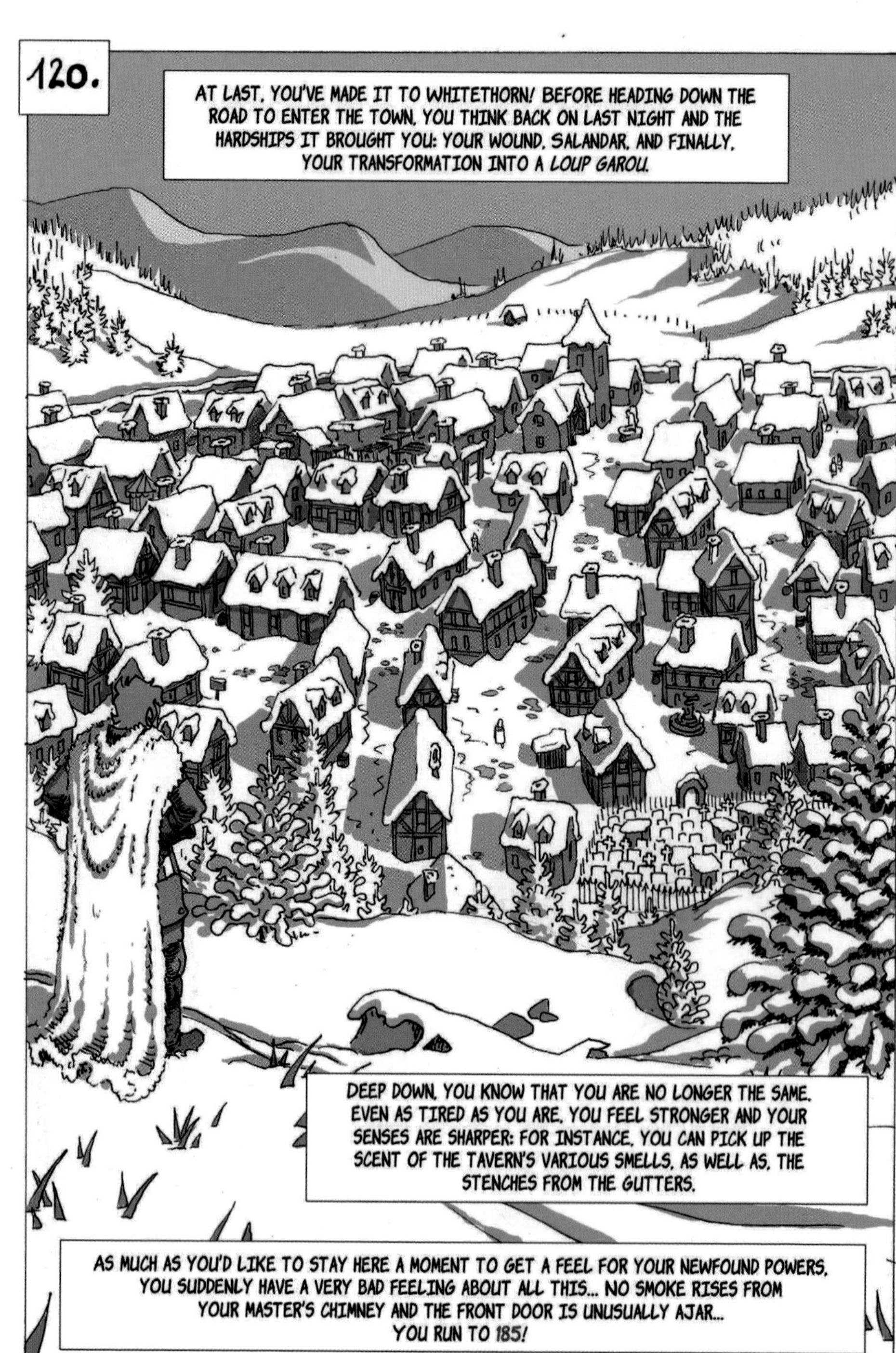
120.
AT LAST, YOU'VE MADE IT TO WHITETHORN! BEFORE HEADING DOWN THE ROAD TO ENTER THE TOWN, YOU THINK BACK ON LAST NIGHT AND THE HARDSHIPS IT BROUGHT YOU: YOUR WOUND, SALANDAR, AND FINALLY, YOUR TRANSFORMATION INTO A *LOUP GAROU*.
DEEP DOWN, YOU KNOW THAT YOU ARE NO LONGER THE SAME. EVEN AS TIRED AS YOU ARE, YOU FEEL STRONGER AND YOUR SENSES ARE SHARPER: FOR INSTANCE, YOU CAN PICK UP THE SCENT OF THE TAVERN'S VARIOUS SMELLS, AS WELL AS, THE STENCHES FROM THE GUTTERS.
AS MUCH AS YOU'D LIKE TO STAY HERE A MOMENT TO GET A FEEL FOR YOUR NEWFOUND POWERS, YOU SUDDENLY HAVE A VERY BAD FEELING ABOUT ALL THIS... NO SMOKE RISES FROM YOUR MASTER'S CHIMNEY AND THE FRONT DOOR IS UNUSUALLY AJAR... YOU RUN TO 185!

## 121.

YESTERDAY MORNING, KALZ THE NOTARY WAS FOUND LIFELESS NEAR THE TEMPLE. STRANGE RUMORS ABOUND: OTHER BODIES HAVE BEEN FOUND TOO. OH! I HOPE WITH ALL MY HEART THAT NOTHING HAS HAPPENED TO THEDOCRED! EORAS, YOU MUST FIND HIM.

HERE, TAKE THIS MAP, USE IT TO FIND YOUR WAY AROUND TOWN! MAYBE YOU SHOULD START NEAR THE MONASTERY. SINCE THE FIRST SNOW, A STRANGE EPIDEMIC HAS BEFALLEN THE TOWN. THE MONKS HAVE OPENED A ROOM WHERE THE ILL CAN GO FOR CARE. IT'S POSSIBLE YOU MAY FIND THEDOCRED THERE.

YOUR INVESTIGATION BEGINS NOW!
GO TO 180 TO CHECK THE MAP.

## 122.

270

21

68

123.

THANK YOU SO MUCH! I WAS AFRAID THAT SOMEONE MIGHT HAVE ROBBED ME, BUT I SEE THAT ALL IS WHERE IT SHOULD BE! HERE, TAKE THESE 15 GP AS MY THANKS.

PROUD OF YOURSELF, YOU HEAD BACK TO THE STREET IN 173.

124.
53

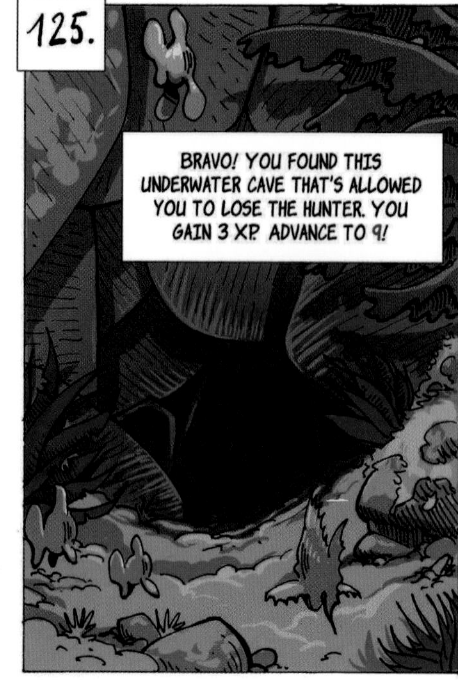
125.
BRAVO! YOU FOUND THIS UNDERWATER CAVE THAT'S ALLOWED YOU TO LOSE THE HUNTER. YOU GAIN 3 XP. ADVANCE TO 9!

126.

THE WOODEN DOOR FINALLY OPENS! YOU CAN ENTER THE CASTLE IN 279.

127.

320

56

TO RETURN TO THE TUNNEL, USE THE DOOR BEHIND YOU IN 72. YOU MAY ALSO SPEAK WITH THESE LADIES.

# 128.

TO TAKE A LOOK IN THE AUTOPSY ROOM, GO TO 39. IF, AND ONLY IF, YOU ACQUIRED A MORGUE EMPLOYEE UNIFORM, YOU MAY GET CLOSE TO THE DESK IN 272 TO READ THE REPORT AND GRAB THE PURSE CONTAINING 10 GP. TO EXIT THE BUILDING, GO TO 62.

# 129.

HELLO, HELLO! ARE YOU INTERESTED IN SOME OF MY WARES, TRAVELLER?

- STEEL HELM (+1 DEFENSE): 20 GP
- DAGGER (+1 STRENGTH): 20 GP
- BOTTLE: 10 GP
- GRAPPLING HOOK: 10 GP
- SAUSAGE (+1 HIT POINT): 3 GP
- SACRED AMULET (+2 MAGIC POINTS AFTER EACH COMBAT WON): 25 GP
- REBIRTH RING (+2 HIT POINTS AFTER EACH COMBAT WON): 25 GP
- SCHOLAR'S BAG (15 SLOTS): 10 GP
- SNAKE WINE (+5 HP): 35 GP
- JADE AMULET: 25 GP

ONCE YOU'RE DONE SHOPPING, RETURN TO 147.

130.

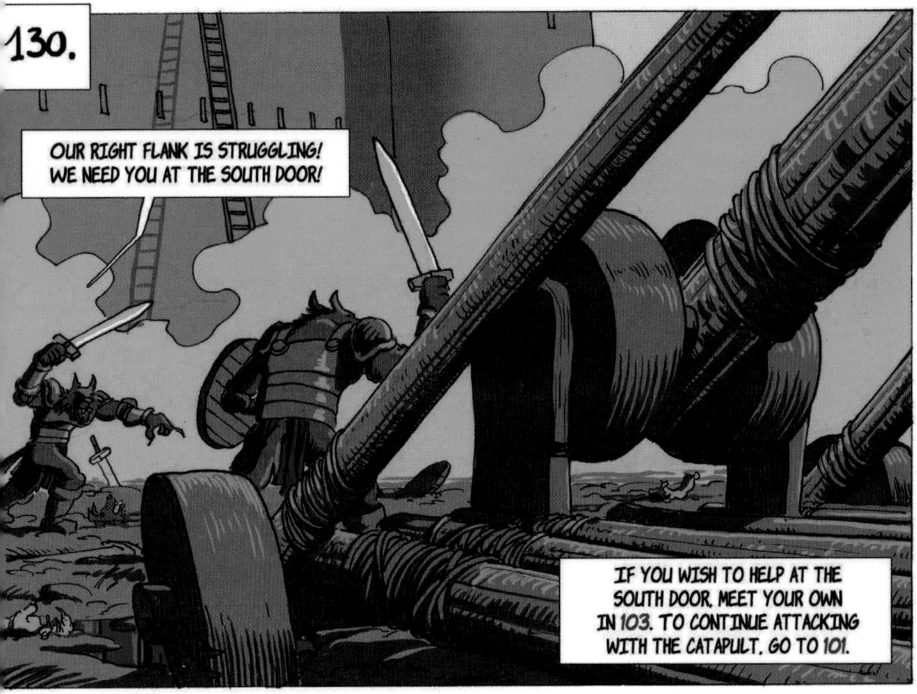

OUR RIGHT FLANK IS STRUGGLING! WE NEED YOU AT THE SOUTH DOOR!

IF YOU WISH TO HELP AT THE SOUTH DOOR, MEET YOUR OWN IN 103. TO CONTINUE ATTACKING WITH THE CATAPULT, GO TO 101.

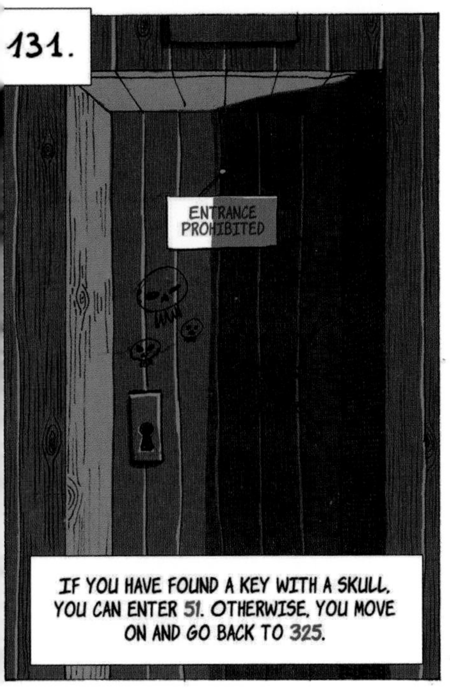
131.
ENTRANCE
PROHIBITED
IF YOU HAVE FOUND A KEY WITH A SKULL, YOU CAN ENTER 51. OTHERWISE, YOU MOVE ON AND GO BACK TO 325.

132.
YOU FOUND MY BAG?
IF YOU HAVE, FOLLOW MADAM MILANN TO 123. OTHERWISE, GO BACK TO 173.

## 133.

SMELLING THE CONTENT OF THE VIAL, YOU BELIEVE YOU RECOGNIZE THE VERY DISTINCTIVE SCENT OF MOUNTAIN BERRIES, A SMALL FRUIT OFTEN USED IN DEFENSE POTIONS. YOU DRINK ITS CONTENT AND GAIN 1 DEFENSE POINT AND 2 HIT POINTS.

RETURN TO 256.

## 134.

YOU MUST BE WONDERING WHAT I'M DOING IN TOWN! I'M INVESTIGATING WEREWOLF DISAPPEARANCES. SINCE MOST OF THEM LIVE HERE, I WAS HOPING TO FIND SOME CLUES. MAYBE WE CAN SHARE WHAT WE FOUND? HERE IS WHAT I COULD DIG UP...

IF YOU ARE IN WEREWOLF FORM, GO TO 291. OTHERWISE, GO TO 205.

## 135.

TURTLE FORMATION! HEAD FOR THE RAMPARTS!

WITHOUT HESITATION, YOU RUN TOWARDS OLDRAK. SHIELD IN HAND, YOU HOLD IT ABOVE YOUR HEAD AND MOVE WITH YOUR WEREWOLF BRETHREN TOWARDS THE RAMPARTS IN 243!

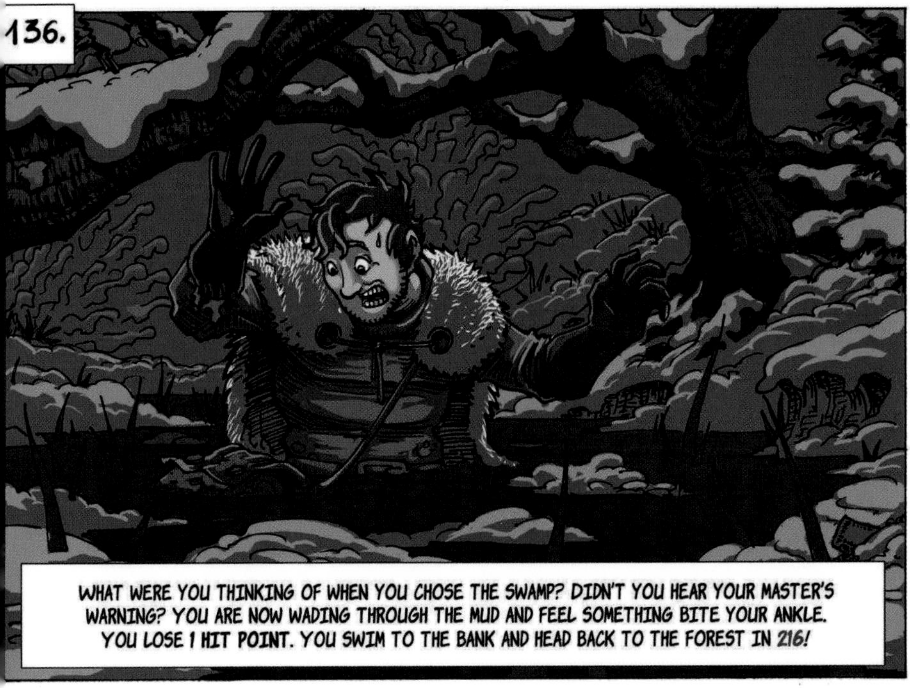

136.

WHAT WERE YOU THINKING OF WHEN YOU CHOSE THE SWAMP? DIDN'T YOU HEAR YOUR MASTER'S WARNING? YOU ARE NOW WADING THROUGH THE MUD AND FEEL SOMETHING BITE YOUR ANKLE. YOU LOSE 1 HIT POINT. YOU SWIM TO THE BANK AND HEAD BACK TO THE FOREST IN 216!

137.

PROJECTILE STRAIGHT AHEAD! HOLD ON TIGHT!

YOU'VE JUST CLIMBED UP AND A PROJECTILE IS HEADING STRAIGHT FOR YOU. YOU CAN JUMP TO THE GROUND TO AVOID IT IN 296, OR HOLD ON TIGHT TO THE SIDE IN 253 AND HOPE THE MISSLE WILL ONLY SCRAPE THE SIEGE ENGINE.

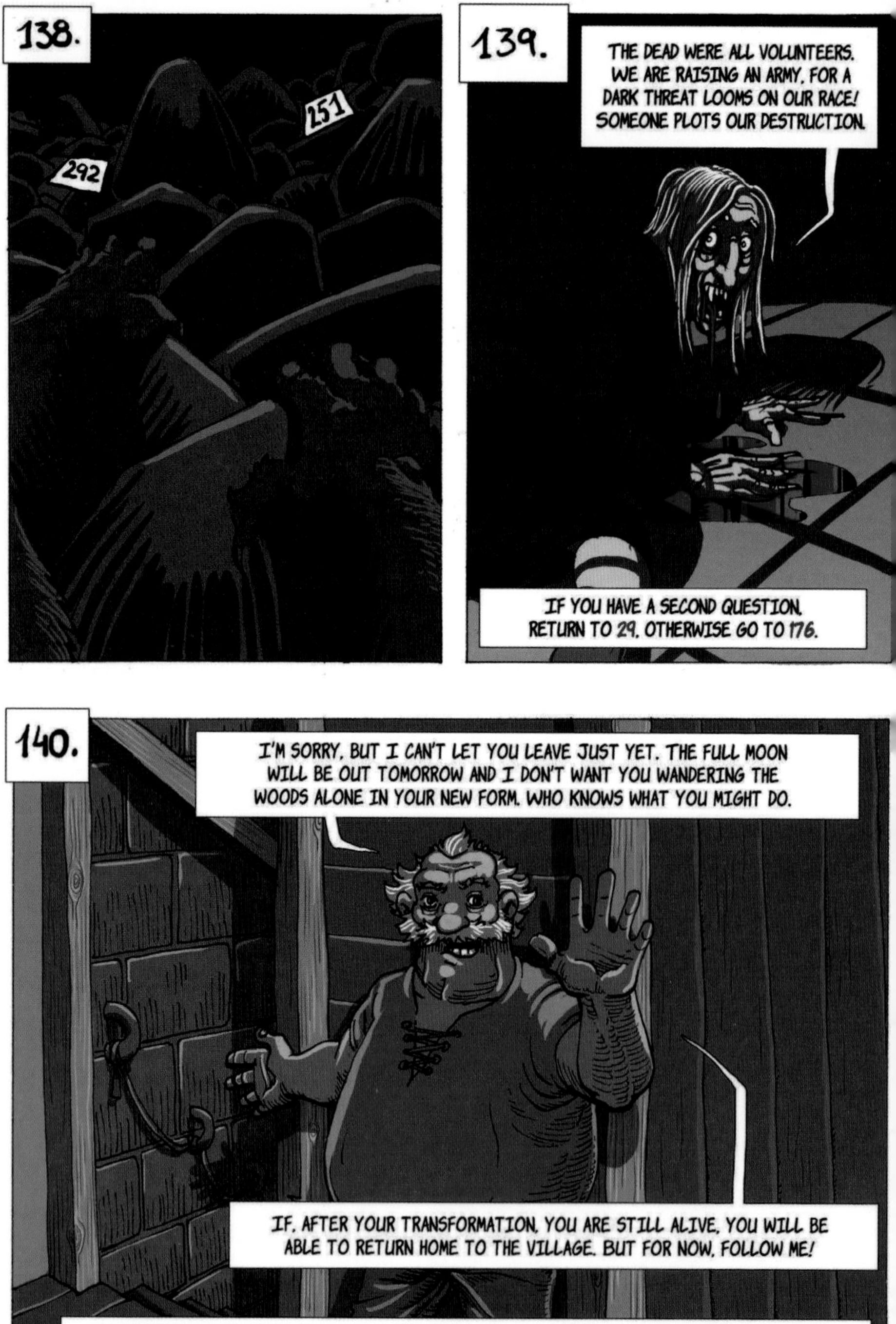

138.
251
292

139.
THE DEAD WERE ALL VOLUNTEERS. WE ARE RAISING AN ARMY, FOR A DARK THREAT LOOMS ON OUR RACE! SOMEONE PLOTS OUR DESTRUCTION.
IF YOU HAVE A SECOND QUESTION, RETURN TO 29. OTHERWISE GO TO 176.

140.

I'M SORRY, BUT I CAN'T LET YOU LEAVE JUST YET. THE FULL MOON WILL BE OUT TOMORROW AND I DON'T WANT YOU WANDERING THE WOODS ALONE IN YOUR NEW FORM. WHO KNOWS WHAT YOU MIGHT DO.

IF, AFTER YOUR TRANSFORMATION, YOU ARE STILL ALIVE, YOU WILL BE ABLE TO RETURN HOME TO THE VILLAGE. BUT FOR NOW, FOLLOW ME!

IT SEEMS THAT YOU HAVE NO CHOICE: YOU MUST FOLLOW GAROLF TO THE LOWER LEVEL IN 84.

## 141.

IT IS NOW TIME TO JOIN THE OTHERS AT THE QUARRY IN 277.

## 142.

38

310

232

15

WELL, YOU CHOSE TO IGNORE THE SIGNS AND ENTER THE HOUSE! COUNT YOURSELF LUCKY, THE OWNER ISN'T HOME!

## 143.

187
240
309

## 144.

CONGRATULATIONS! BY ENTERING THIS TUNNEL, YOU'VE OUTWITTED THE HUNTER. YOU GAIN 3 XP. YOU MAY CONTINUE ON YOUR WAY AND PROGRESS TO 72.

## 145.

WE ARE NOT INTERESTED IN WHATEVER YOU ARE SELLING! GO AWAY!
THE OWNER REFUSES TO OPEN THE DOOR! RETURN TO 173.

## 146.

YOU MAY ONLY CHOOSE ONE: THE POTION THAT GRANTS 2 HIT POINTS, THE ONE THAT GRANTS 2 MAGIC POINTS, OR THE INVISIBILITY POTION. ONCE YOU'VE MADE YOUR CHOICE, RETURN TO 322.

147.
429
38
223

148.
RIDICULOUS! I HAVE BEEN WAITING FOR AN HOUR AND I STILL HAVE NOT BEEN CALLED ON!
YOU WON'T LEARN ANYTHING ELSE FROM THIS PATIENT. RETURN TO THE HALL IN 201.

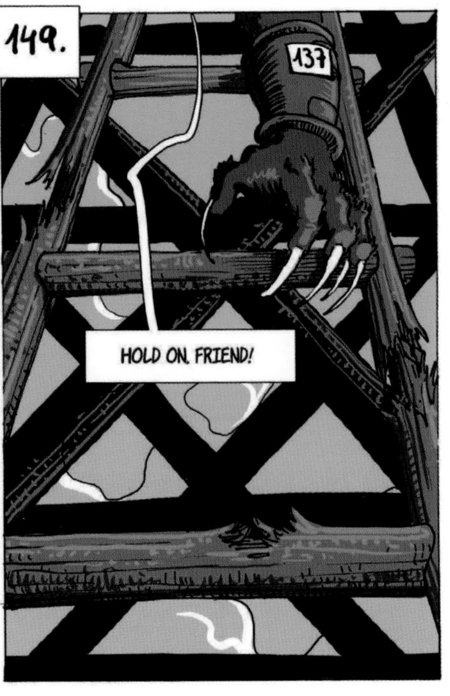
149.
137
HOLD ON, FRIEND!

150.
DUKE MCKINLEY IS VERY WORRIED, WILLIAM. ACCORDING TO RUMOR, WEREWOLVES HAVE STARTED DISAPPEARING MYSTERIOUSLY!
YOU STRUGGLE TO HEAR THE MAN'S ANSWER. YOU MOVE A LITTLE CLOSER IN 225.

151.

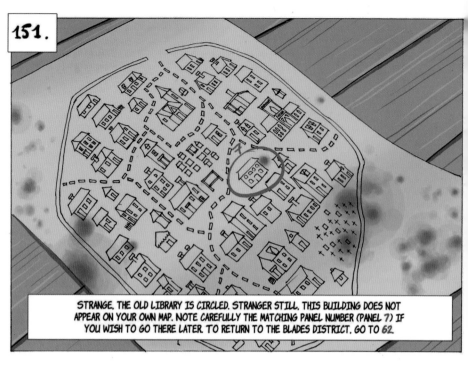

STRANGE, THE OLD LIBRARY IS CIRCLED. STRANGER STILL, THIS BUILDING DOES NOT APPEAR ON YOUR OWN MAP. NOTE CAREFULLY THE MATCHING PANEL NUMBER (PANEL 7) IF YOU WISH TO GO THERE LATER. TO RETURN TO THE BLADES DISTRICT, GO TO 62.

152.
NOW THAT YOU KNOW HOW TO FIGHT, GAROLF HAS ALLOWED YOU TO EXPLORE HIS HOUSE. YOU CAN READ HIS BOOKS IN 25, VISIT HIS KITCHEN IN 209, OR EXPLORE THE HALLWAY IN 325.

153.
YOU FIND A FLASK THAT GIVES 1 HIT POINT. THE CHEST TO YOUR RIGHT IS LOCKED. IF YOU HAVE THE "STREET THIEF" SKILL, OPEN IT AND GAIN A RING THAT GRANTS +2 STRENGTH.
NOW, RETURN TO 240!

154.
I HAVE YOU, FOUL BEAST!
YOU WERE FOOLISH TO WALK AROUND TOWN AS A WEREWOLF, IN BROAD DAYLIGHT NO LESS! YOUR ADVENTURE ENDS HERE. RESTART AT 1.

155.
THE LADDER IS BROKEN – YOU'LL NEVER REACH THE TOP OF THE RAMPARTS! GO BACK DOWN TO 300 AND CHOOSE ANOTHER ONE!

156.
YOU COME FACE TO FACE WITH AN ASH HOUND. HE DOES NOT APPEAR TO WANT TO ATTACK YOU, BUT HE'S BLOCKING YOUR WAY. YOU CAN TRY TO COAX HIM IN 8, OR TURN BACK AROUND AND HEAD TOWARDS THE FARM IN 47.

157.
YOU'VE BARELY TAKEN TWO STEPS BEFORE ARROWS START RAINING DOWN ALL AROUND YOU. TO SURVIVE, YOU CAN TRY TO HIDE UNDER A SHIELD THAT WAS LEFT ON THE GROUND IN 88, OR RUN TOWARDS THE SIEGE TOWER IN 248.

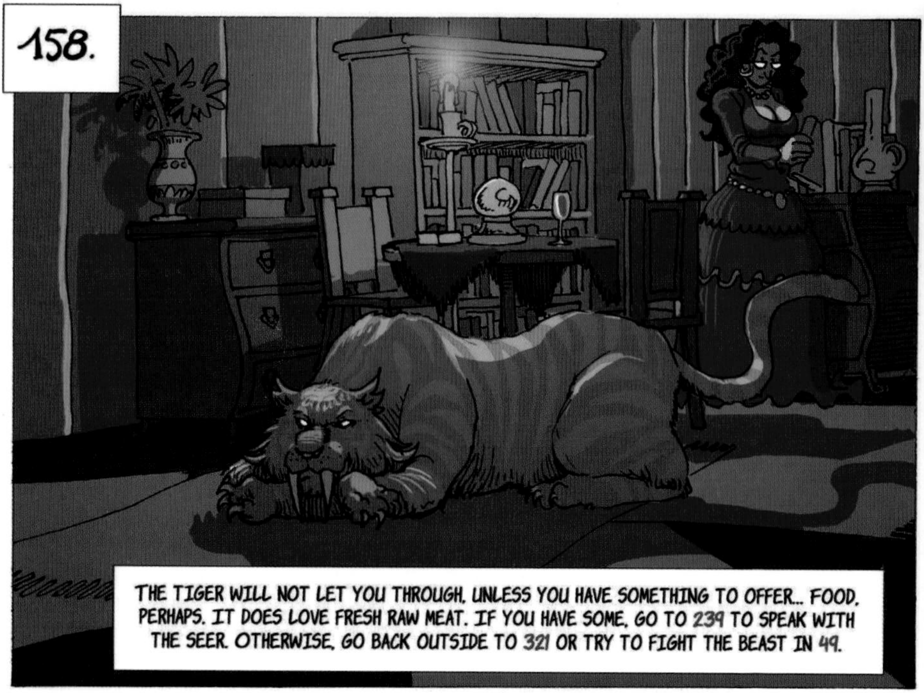

## 158.

THE TIGER WILL NOT LET YOU THROUGH, UNLESS YOU HAVE SOMETHING TO OFFER... FOOD, PERHAPS. IT DOES LOVE FRESH RAW MEAT. IF YOU HAVE SOME, GO TO 239 TO SPEAK WITH THE SEER. OTHERWISE, GO BACK OUTSIDE TO 321 OR TRY TO FIGHT THE BEAST IN 49.

## 159.

VAMPIRE
STRENGTH: 13
HIT POINTS: 19
LOOT: 1 SHIELD THAT GRANTS 1 DEFENSE POINT
XP EARNED: 5
TREMBLE, WOLF!
HERE IS YOUR FIRST ENEMY. AFTER DEFEATING HIM, CHOOSE WHICH WAY TO GO. DO YOU TRY TO GO AROUND THE VAMPIRES TO QUICKLY REACH THE RAMPARTS IN 48, OR WILL YOU RUN HEAD FIRST INTO THE BATTLE IN 103?

## 160.

FRESH WATER HARPY
STRENGTH: 6
HIT POINTS: 13
LOOT: 5 GP AND A POTION THAT GRANTS 2 MAGIC POINTS
XP EARNED: 4
IF YOU WIN THE COMBAT, TAKE THE LOOT. DON'T FORGET TO WRITE DOWN THOSE BONUSES ON YOUR CHARACTER SHEET!
NOW, TAKE THE PATH IN 147.

## 161.

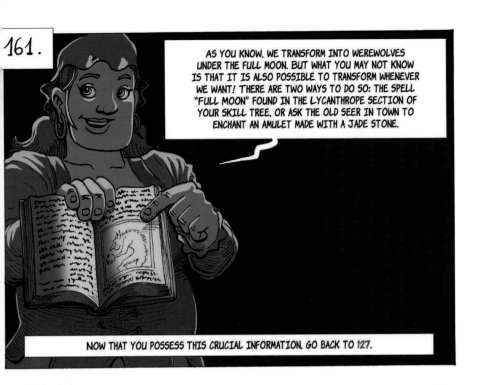

AS YOU KNOW, WE TRANSFORM INTO WEREWOLVES UNDER THE FULL MOON. BUT WHAT YOU MAY NOT KNOW IS THAT IT IS ALSO POSSIBLE TO TRANSFORM WHENEVER WE WANT! THERE ARE TWO WAYS TO DO SO: THE SPELL "FULL MOON" FOUND IN THE LYCANTHROPE SECTION OF YOUR SKILL TREE, OR ASK THE OLD SEER IN TOWN TO ENCHANT AN AMULET MADE WITH A JADE STONE.

NOW THAT YOU POSSESS THIS CRUCIAL INFORMATION, GO BACK TO 127.

## 162.

HURRAY FOR EORAS!
THERE'S NO TIME TO LOSE : CLIMB THE SIEGE TOWER!
THE CHOICE IS YOURS: EITHER CLIMB THE SIEGE TOWER IN 137, OR CONTINUE ON THE BATTLEFIELD IN 3.

## 163.

YOU'VE JUST FOUND A MAGICAL VIAL THAT ALLOWS YOU TO GAIN 1 MAGIC POINT AND 1 HIT POINT. RETURN TO 276!

164.
NOTHING INTERESTING HERE REALLY.
RETRACE YOUR STEPS IN 303.

165.
MORGUE
214

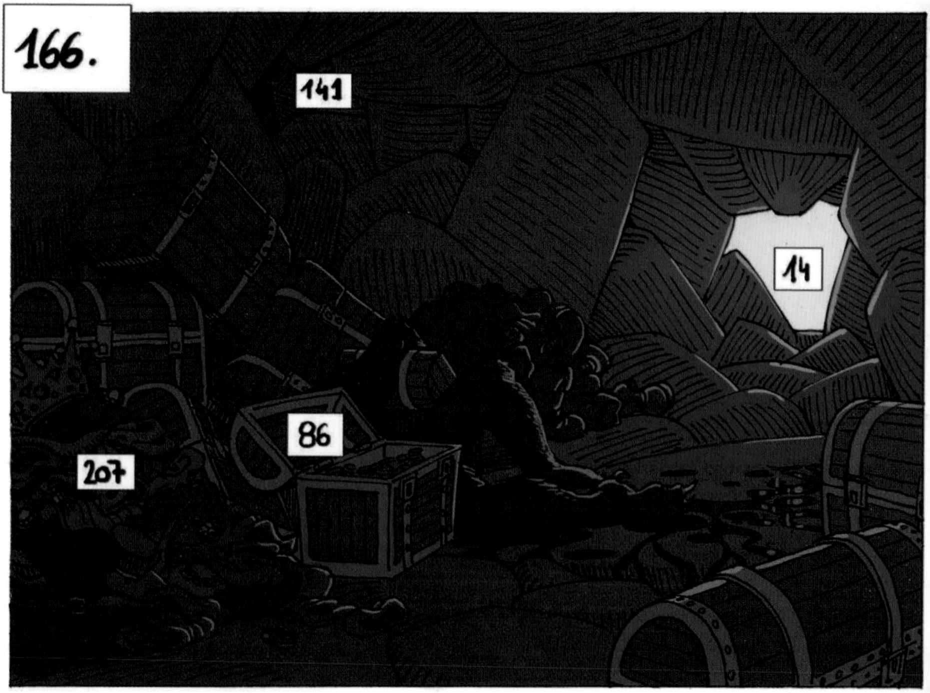

166.

141

14

86

207

# 167.

AH, THE THREE PHEASANTS TAVERN! IT HAS ALWAYS FELT LIKE HOME. THE OWNER IS A CHILDHOOD COMPANION AND THE PATRONS TRUE FRIENDS. BUT SADLY, THERE'S NO TIME FOR FRIVOLITY, YOU MUST FIND THEDOCRED!

250

324

197

TO EXIT THE INN, GO TO 318.

# 168.

HALT! NONE MAY PASS!

I HAVE AN IDEA: I'LL DISTRACT HIM WHILE YOU SNEAK INTO THE TENT THROUGH THE BACK IN 322. WE'LL MEET UP AT DUSK IN THE QUARRY.

YOU CAN ALSO TURN AROUND AND GO BACK TO 104.

169.

260

231

23

170.

EORAS! COME HELP US! THE ENEMY CATAPULT PERCHED ON THE RAMPART IS CAUSING TOO MUCH DAMAGE! WE MUST DESTROY IT!
YOU CAN BRING THE STONE FOUND AT YOUR FEET IN 323.
OR TAKE CARE OF THIS TROLL WHO'S DELAYING US IN 33.

171.
YOUR MASTER IS IN OUR HEADQUARTERS. THE OLD CASTLE HIDDEN IN THE FOREST. BUT HE IS NOT HELD THERE AGAINST HIS WILL...
IF YOU HAVE A SECOND QUESTION, RETURN TO 29. OTHERWISE, GO TO 176.

172.
YOU ARE HIT WITH SUCH FORCE THAT YOU LAND IN THE MOAT IN 11, OVER 15 FEET AWAY.

173.

VINUS
10
145
132

TO RETURN TO THE MISTS DISTRICT SQUARE, GO TO 315.

174.

MY FALCONS ARE AS FAST AS LIGHTNING AND AS STRONG AS THUNDER! WOULD YOU LIKE OWNING ONE? THEY ONLY COST 20 GP EACH...

COMBAT FALCON

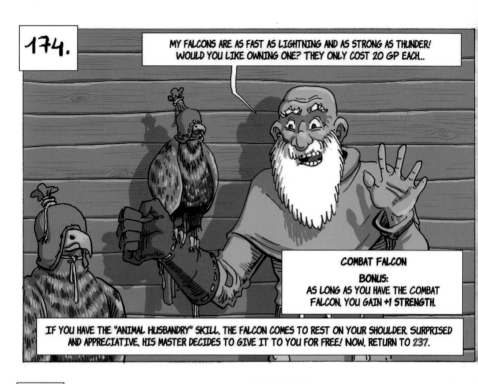

BONUS:
AS LONG AS YOU HAVE THE COMBAT FALCON, YOU GAIN +1 STRENGTH.

IF YOU HAVE THE "ANIMAL HUSBANDRY" SKILL, THE FALCON COMES TO REST ON YOUR SHOULDER. SURPRISED AND APPRECIATIVE, HIS MASTER DECIDES TO GIVE IT TO YOU FOR FREE! NOW, RETURN TO 237.

175.

HEY, A NEW PERSON TO SKIN!
ROBBER
STRENGTH: 5
HIT POINTS: 11
LOOT: 15 GP
XP EARNED: 3

IF YOU DEFEAT THE ROBBER, YOU CAN EITHER KEEP THE 15 GOLD PIECES AND CONTINUE ON YOUR WAY IN 316, OR GIVE THE PIECES BACK TO THE YOUNG WOMAN IN 109.

176.

THESE REVELATIONS ARE SURPRISING! WE SHOULD INFORM OLDRAK, THE LEADER OF MY PACK! I'M CERTAIN HE WILL HELP US. HE'S ALSO INVESTIGATING THE WEREWOLF DISAPPEARANCES. MAYBE HE KNOWS SOMETHING ABOUT THEDOCRED! FOLLOW ME OUTSIDE TO 134!

BE SURE TO CHANGE BACK INTO A HUMAN, WEREWOLF HUNTERS ARE LURKING AROUND.

177.

72

178.

CAN'T YOU SEE THAT WE'RE WORKING HERE?
THESE NURSES DO NOT APPEAR TO WANT TO HELP YOU. GO BACK TO 21.

179.

12

287

ONCE OUTSIDE, YOU TAKE A DEEP BREATH AND LET THE FRESH AIR FILL YOUR LUNGS.

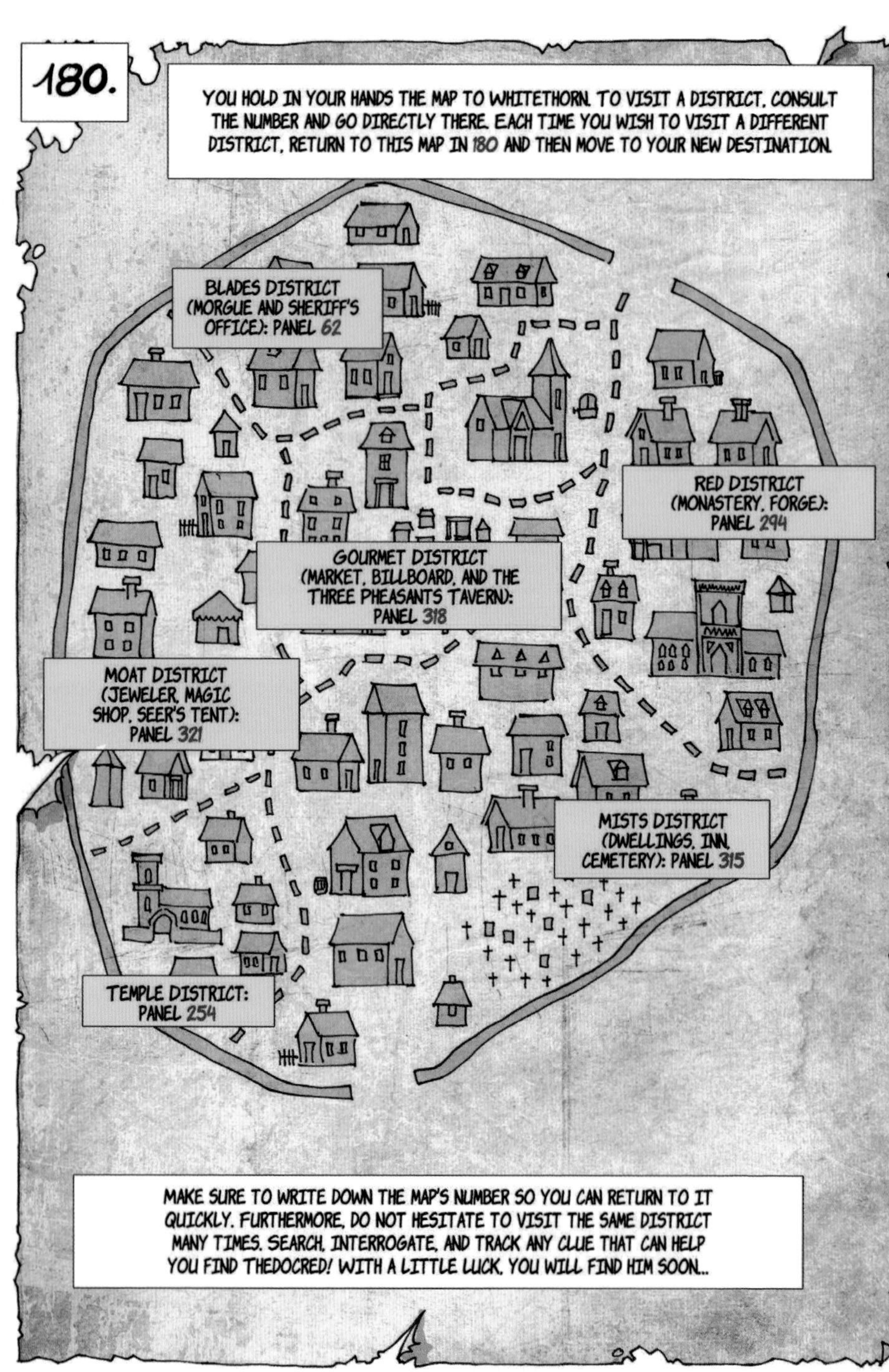
180.
YOU HOLD IN YOUR HANDS THE MAP TO WHITETHORN. TO VISIT A DISTRICT, CONSULT THE NUMBER AND GO DIRECTLY THERE. EACH TIME YOU WISH TO VISIT A DIFFERENT DISTRICT, RETURN TO THIS MAP IN 180 AND THEN MOVE TO YOUR NEW DESTINATION.
BLADES DISTRICT (MORGUE AND SHERIFF'S OFFICE): PANEL 62
RED DISTRICT (MONASTERY, FORGE): PANEL 294
GOURMET DISTRICT (MARKET, BILLBOARD, AND THE THREE PHEASANTS TAVERN): PANEL 318
MOAT DISTRICT (JEWELER, MAGIC SHOP, SEER'S TENT): PANEL 321
MISTS DISTRICT (DWELLINGS, INN, CEMETERY): PANEL 315
TEMPLE DISTRICT: PANEL 254
MAKE SURE TO WRITE DOWN THE MAP'S NUMBER SO YOU CAN RETURN TO IT QUICKLY. FURTHERMORE, DO NOT HESITATE TO VISIT THE SAME DISTRICT MANY TIMES. SEARCH, INTERROGATE, AND TRACK ANY CLUE THAT CAN HELP YOU FIND THEDOCRED! WITH A LITTLE LUCK, YOU WILL FIND HIM SOON...

# 181.

177

12

# 182.

TWO NIGHTS AGO, I SAW OLDRAK SNEAK OUT OF THE CAMP FOLLOWED BY HIS RIGHT HAND MAN, JASTOK. WHEN THEY CAME BACK AT THE CRACK OF DAWN, THEY WERE BOTH CARRYING FULL BAGS. AT FIRST, I THOUGHT THEY WERE BRINGING BACK GAME, BUT THEN I SAW THIS GOLD PIECE FALL OUT OF ONE OF THE BAGS. SINCE THEN, THEIR TENT IS GUARDED AND NO ONE CAN GET INSIDE IT.

STRANGE INDEED...

I HOPE THAT MY BROTHER IS ALIVE. IF YOU EVER SEE HIM, HE WEARS A PENDANT THAT IS VERY HARD TO FORGET: A BIG HEART-SHAPED GEM WITH THE LETTERS "E. M" ENGRAVED ON IT. HIS FIANCÉE'S INITIALS!

GO TO 281.

183.

Made of iron,
it is also gold.
It gives time
to music and
raises standards.

STRANGE... IF YOU KNOW THE ANSWER TO THIS RIDDLE, GO TO 98; OTHERWISE, GO BACK TO 64.

184.
YOU MUST NOW LOOK FOR THE SECOND KEY. IF YOU HAVEN'T YET FOUND IT, RETURN TO 78.

185.
YOU WERE RIGHT TO WORRY: THE FRONT DOOR HAS BEEN SMASHED OPEN. WEAPON DRAWN, YOU DECIDE TO CAREFULLY ENTER IN 60.

186.

OLDRAK, WHEN EORAS AND I INFILTRATED THE MCKINLEY'S LAIR IN WHITETHORN, WE CLEARLY HEARD THEM SAY THEY WERE NOT RESPONSIBLE FOR THE WEREWOLF ABDUCTIONS! IF WE ATTACK THEM, WE—

YOU MUST HAVE MISUNDERSTOOD THEM! THESE VAMPIRES ARE THE CAUSE OF ALL OF OUR TROUBLES, AND THEY WILL PAY DEARLY! BOTH OF YOU, GET READY. WE WILL MEET AT THE QUARRY IN AN HOUR!

OLDRAK IS SET ON ATTACKING THE VAMPIRES AND IGNORES YOUR ARGUMENTS. JOIN HIM AT THE CAMP IN 237.

187.

VAMPIRE

STRENGTH: 16
HIT POINTS: 30
LOOT: NONE
XP EARNED: 5

IF YOU WIN THE COMBAT, YOU MAY ENTER THE WEAPONS ROOM IN 81. IF YOU DIED DURING THE COMBAT, RETURN TO PANEL 1!

188.
FENNEL ROE DEER (FOR FOUR WEREWOLVES)
BEFORE PUTTING YOUR MEAT ON THE SPIT,
BASTE GENEROUSLY WITH OIL
AND RUB WITH FENNEL.
ADD SALT AND PEPPER TO TASTE.
PREPARE YOUR CAMPFIRE.
WAIT UNTIL THE FLAMES BURN
A BRIGHT RED.
THEN COOK FOR SEVENTY-FIVE MINUTES
FOR A RARE TREAT. REMOVE FROM THE FIRE
AND SERVE WITH SOME MUSHROOMS!
BON APPÉTIT!
AFTER YOU ARE DONE READING, GO TO 25.

189.
YOU FIND YOURSELF RELAXED AFTER THIS BRIEF MEDITATION. YOU FEEL BETTER AND REGAIN 1 HIT POINT. NOTE THAT THIS PANEL WILL NO LONGER BE AVAILABLE! RETURN TO THE HALL IN 46.

190.
YOUR DIVERSION WORKED - THE GUARD DOES NOT SEE YOU COME OUT IN 261. HOWEVER, THE SMOKE PREVENTS YOU FROM BREATHING NORMALLY AND YOU LOSE 1 HIT POINT.

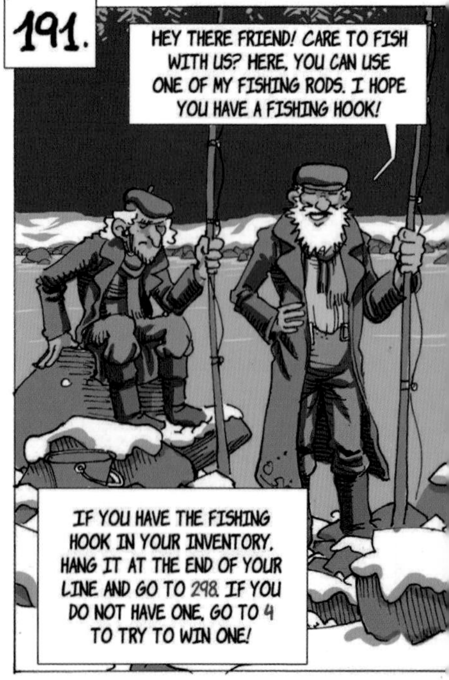
191.
HEY THERE FRIEND! CARE TO FISH WITH US? HERE, YOU CAN USE ONE OF MY FISHING RODS. I HOPE YOU HAVE A FISHING HOOK!
IF YOU HAVE THE FISHING HOOK IN YOUR INVENTORY, HANG IT AT THE END OF YOUR LINE AND GO TO 298. IF YOU DO NOT HAVE ONE, GO TO 4 TO TRY TO WIN ONE!

192.
YOUR ADVENTURE ENDS HERE, MONSTER!
THE HUNTER SLITS YOUR THROAT WITHOUT ANY PITY. TO RESTART, GO TO PANEL 1.

193.
THIS CURIOUS CREATURE IS LYONA: HALF-WOMAN, HALF-SPIDER! IF YOU DEFEAT HER, THE KEY IS YOURS!
LYONA
STRENGTH: 17
HIT POINTS: 25
LOOT: THE KEY
XP EARNED: 4
IF YOU WIN THIS COMBAT, RETURN TO 21 WITH THE KEY.

194.

118

WARNING! QUICKSAND 305

## 195.

I DON'T WANT ANY RUNAWAYS IN MY PACK! I'M GIVING YOU ONE LAST CHANCE: GO BACK TO THE BATTLE AND PROVE TO ME THAT YOU AREN'T A COWARD!
YOU PICK UP YOUR FALLEN WEAPON AND REJOIN YOUR BROTHERS IN ARMS IN 172.

## 196.

ASH HOUND
BONUS:
ADD 1 TO YOUR STRENGTH AND 1 TO YOUR DEFENSE.
CONGRATULATIONS, THIS ASH HOUND IS NOW YOURS! READ ITS BONUS ABILITY WELL, IT WILL BE VERY USEFUL. YOU CAN RELEASE YOUR COMPANION AT ANY TIME, BUT NOTE THAT YOU WILL LOSE THE BENEFITS IT GRANTS. YOU CAN HAVE ONLY ONE COMPANION AT A TIME!
NOW GO TO 47!

## 197.

HELLO EORAS, IT'S BEEN A WHILE! THEDOCRED? NO, I HAVEN'T SEEN HIM, SORRY! I THOUGHT THAT CRAZY OLD FOOL HAD ONCE AGAIN DISAPPEARED INTO HIS WORK.

SADLY, NEOGUINE THE BARMAN WON'T BE ABLE TO TELL YOU MORE, NEITHER WILL ANY OF THE OTHER PATRONS YOU'VE INTERROGATED. GO BACK TO 167.

198.

IT IS TOO LATE EORAS, WE WON'T BE ABLE TO STOP THIS BATTLE! BUT IF THEDOCRED IS INSIDE THE VAMPIRES' CASTLE, WE MUST REACH HIM AS SOON AS POSSIBLE! ONCE INSIDE, MAYBE WE'LL FIND A WAY TO STOP THIS BLOOD BATH! GOOD LUCK MY FRIEND!

IF YOU ARE NOT IN WEREWOLF FORM, IT IS TIME TO TRANSFORM. THE BATTLE WILL BE A TOUGH ONE AND A SIMPLE HUMAN WILL NOT SURVIVE FOR LONG! GO TO 74.

199.

## 200.

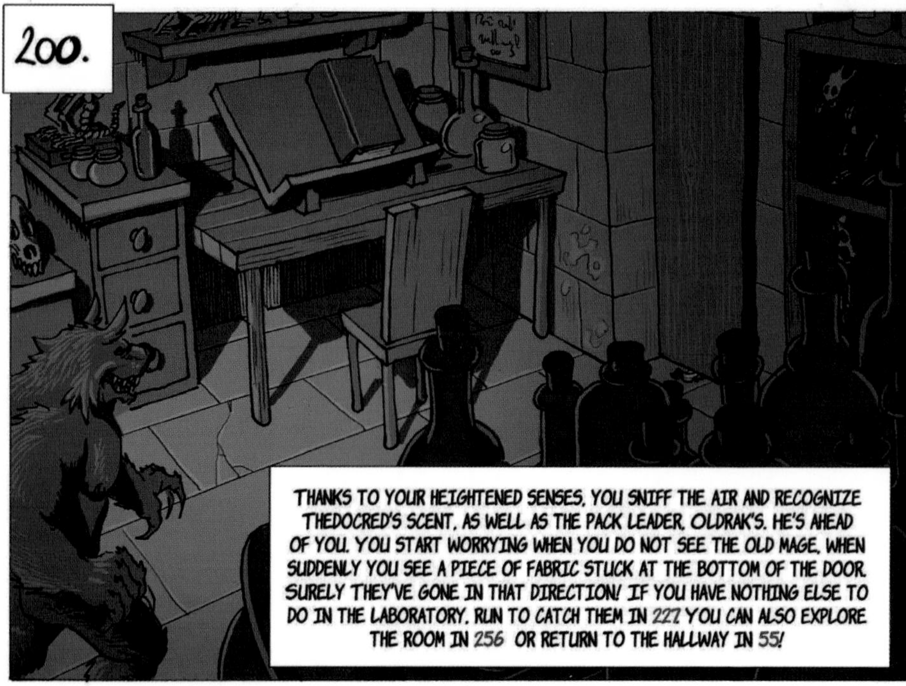

THANKS TO YOUR HEIGHTENED SENSES, YOU SNIFF THE AIR AND RECOGNIZE THEDOCRED'S SCENT, AS WELL AS THE PACK LEADER, OLDRAK'S. HE'S AHEAD OF YOU. YOU START WORRYING WHEN YOU DO NOT SEE THE OLD MAGE, WHEN SUDDENLY YOU SEE A PIECE OF FABRIC STUCK AT THE BOTTOM OF THE DOOR. SURELY THEY'VE GONE IN THAT DIRECTION! IF YOU HAVE NOTHING ELSE TO DO IN THE LABORATORY, RUN TO CATCH THEM IN 227 YOU CAN ALSO EXPLORE THE ROOM IN 256 OR RETURN TO THE HALLWAY IN 55!

## 201.

297

148

43

TO RETURN TO THE STREET, GO TO 294.

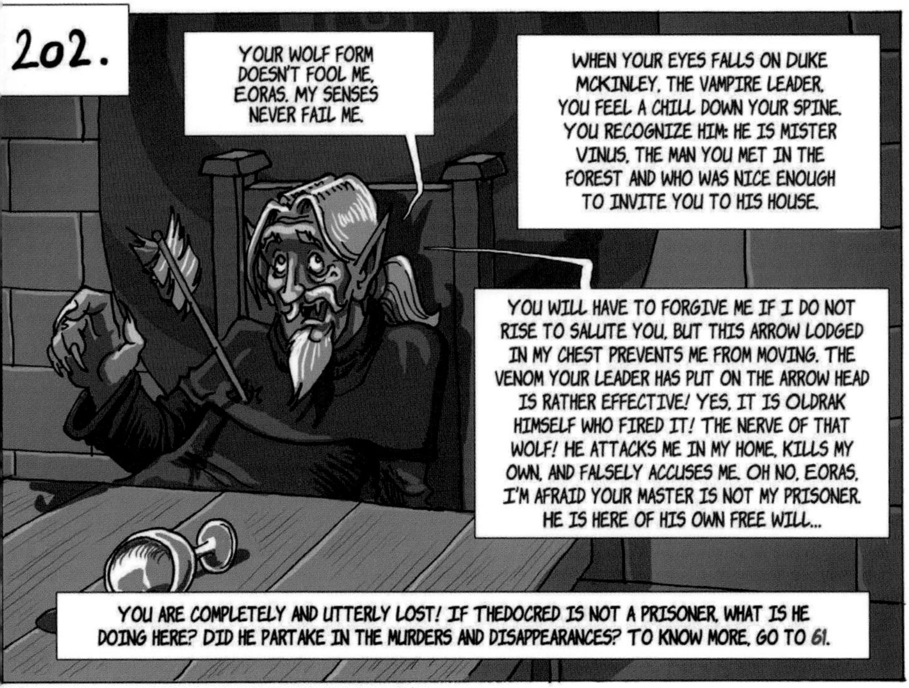

202.

YOUR WOLF FORM DOESN'T FOOL ME, EORAS. MY SENSES NEVER FAIL ME.

WHEN YOUR EYES FALLS ON DUKE MCKINLEY, THE VAMPIRE LEADER, YOU FEEL A CHILL DOWN YOUR SPINE. YOU RECOGNIZE HIM: HE IS MISTER VINUS, THE MAN YOU MET IN THE FOREST AND WHO WAS NICE ENOUGH TO INVITE YOU TO HIS HOUSE.

YOU WILL HAVE TO FORGIVE ME IF I DO NOT RISE TO SALUTE YOU, BUT THIS ARROW LODGED IN MY CHEST PREVENTS ME FROM MOVING. THE VENOM YOUR LEADER HAS PUT ON THE ARROW HEAD IS RATHER EFFECTIVE! YES, IT IS OLDRAK HIMSELF WHO FIRED IT! THE NERVE OF THAT WOLF! HE ATTACKS ME IN MY HOME, KILLS MY OWN, AND FALSELY ACCUSES ME. OH NO, EORAS, I'M AFRAID YOUR MASTER IS NOT MY PRISONER. HE IS HERE OF HIS OWN FREE WILL...

YOU ARE COMPLETELY AND UTTERLY LOST! IF THEDOCRED IS NOT A PRISONER, WHAT IS HE DOING HERE? DID HE PARTAKE IN THE MURDERS AND DISAPPEARANCES? TO KNOW MORE, GO TO 61.

203.
156

204.
252
266

205.
WHEN I GOT INTO TOWN, I HOPED TO FIND MY FRIENDS AT THE MONASTERY, ILL OR WOUNDED, BUT AT LEAST ALIVE. SADLY, NONE OF THEM WERE THERE.

THAT'S WHEN I LEARNT MANY THINGS THAT FUELED MY CURIOSITY: HUMANS WERE ALSO DISAPPEARING. BUT UNLIKE OUR KIND, THEIR BODIES WERE FOUND. STRANGER STILL, THEY HAD ALL BEEN DRAINED OF THEIR BLOOD.

I IMMEDIATELY THOUGHT ABOUT THE VAMPIRES. BUT A QUESTION WAS TROUBLING ME: WHY SO MANY VICTIMS? WAS IT A FAMISHED VAMPIRE, OR WORSE, A CLAN THAT WAS RECRUITING...?

ALAS, THIS LAST HYPOTHESIS PROVED TO BE CORRECT. WHEN I SAW THE GRAVES IN THE CEMETARY, I KNEW THAT SOMEONE WAS NOT UNEARTHING THE DEAD! NO, THE DEAD THEMSELVES WERE AWAKENING...

AT THAT TIME, I STILL HADN'T LEARNED ANYTHING ABOUT THE DISAPPEARANCES OF MY CLANSMEN. HOWEVER, I HAD TO SHARE THESE DISCOVERIES WITH MY LEADER AS SOON AS POSSIBLE. IF THE VAMPIRES WERE RECRUITING, THE PACK NEEDED TO PREPARE.
I WAS ABOUT TO HEAD OUT WHEN YOU ENTERED THE OLD LIBRARY. WHEN I NOTICED THE RED SPIRAL, THE OLD MCKINLEY VAMPIRE CLAN'S SYMBOL, I KNEW RIGHT AWAY THAT YOU WERE ALSO INVESTIGATING. THUS, I FOLLOWED YOU...AND YOU KNOW THE REST.
GO TO 102.

206.
66
311
FEEL FREE TO TAKE A LOOK AT THESE SIGNS. WHO KNOWS, THEY MAY BE VERY INTERESTING. YOU CAN ALSO RETURN TO THE GOURMET DISTRICT SQUARE IN 318.

207.
GO BACK TO 166.

208.

157

117

## 209.

IT SEEMS THAT YOU'VE RUN INTO ONE OF GAROLF'S CHILDREN. YOU CAN GO MEET HIM IN 282, KEEP EXPLORING THE BACK KITCHEN IN 105, OR GO BACK TO THE PREVIOUS ROOM IN 152.

## 210.

HAVE MERCY!

GAROLF AND MISTER VINUS CAME TO YOUR RESCUE. THEY HANDLED SALANDAR WHILE YOU WERE BUSY WITH OLDRAK. AFTER YOUR VICTORY, YOU TIE HIM UP SECURELY AND PUT HIM IN A CAGE WITH HIS ACCOMPLICE IN 314.

## 211.

118
194

## 212.

STONE GIANT
STRENGTH: 7
HIT POINTS: 20
LOOT: NONE
XP EARNED: 5
SILLY WELP, YOU CAME INTO MY DOMAIN WITHOUT PERMISSION. AND YOU DARE ROB ME? I WILL MASH YOU INTO PULP AND MAKE A BEAUTIFUL NECKLACE WITH YOUR BONES!
IF YOU MAKE IT OUT OF THIS COMBAT ALIVE, YOU CAN RETURN TO THE MILITARY CAMP YARD IN 276. IF YOU RUN OUT OF HIT POINTS, RETURN TO PANEL 1.

## 213.

HAVE I INVESTIGATED THE MURDERS? SADLY NOT. THE SHERIFF ONLY GIVES ME THE DIRTY WORK. AND IF YOU ASK ME, THAT'S WASTING MY TALENTS. I'D BE VERY HANDY IN THE FIELD. FOR EXAMPLE, I KNOW THE SPIRAL MARKS FOUND NEAR THE BODIES BELONG TO AN ANCIENT VAMPIRE CLAN: THE MCKINLEYS!
OH NO... NOT OGRE STEW! EVEN THE RATS WON'T EAT THAT SLOP...
THAT IS VERY INTERESTING INFORMATION. YOU THANK THE WARDEN AND RETURN TO THE HALL IN 220.

## 214.

PASSWORD!?
BLACK WIDOW!
YOU NOW KNOW THE PASSWORD THAT WILL ALLOW YOU TO ENTER THE BUILDING IN 241. IF YOU WISH TO VISIT ANOTHER DISTRICT, LOOK AT YOUR MAP IN 180.

## 215.

YOU SMELL THE ROBE THAT WAS LEFT ON THE FLOOR AND YOU RECOGNIZE, ONCE AGAIN, THEDOCRED'S UNIQUE SCENT. WITHOUT A DOUBT, HE WAS TAKEN ELSEWHERE. THERE'S NOT A MINUTE TO LOSE. RETURN TO THE HALLWAY IN 306.

## 216.

217.

THESE JADE AMULETS ARE NOT CHEAP JUNK – THEY'RE ALREADY ENCHANTED! HOWEVER, AS YOU MAY HAVE GUESSED, THEY ARE RATHER EXPENSIVE. IF YOU WANT ONE, IT WILL COST YOU 1 STRENGTH POINT AND 1 DEFENSE POINT.

THE ABILITY TO TRANSFORM INTO A WEREWOLF OUTSIDE OF A FULL MOON IS ESSENTIAL FOR THE REST OF THIS ADVENTURE. IT'S UP TO YOU TO CHOOSE: PAY THE PRICE, OR LOOK FOR ANOTHER WAY. WHEN YOU'VE DECIDED, GO BACK TO THE STREET IN 254.

218.

I SAW THEM... THESE MONSTERS ATTACK AT NIGHT! THEY HAVE BIG YELLOW EYES AND THEIR TEETH ARE AS SHARP AS BLADES! YOU BELIEVE ME, DON'T YOU?
TIRED, THE PATIENT FALLS ASLEEP. CONTINUE INVESTIGATING IN 297.

219.

YOU, SIR, ARE NOT THE FIRST TO ASK ME ABOUT THESE MURDERS! AND FOR THE UMPTEENTH TIME, I AM NOT AUTHORIZED TO TALK ABOUT IT!
THIS MAN WILL NOT TALK, BUT YOU'RE CONVINCED THAT HE KNOWS SOMETHING THAT COULD HELP YOUR INVESTIGATION. WILL YOU RETRACE YOUR STEPS TO 26, OR WILL YOU TRY TO SHADOW HIM UP TO 124? BE CAREFUL, IF YOU HAVE ALREADY SHADOWED THIS MAN, YOU CANNOT CHOOSE THIS OPTION AGAIN.

## 220

IF YOU'VE KILLED THE WANTED BANDIT, GO GET YOUR REWARD IN 111. IF YOU WANT TO ASK ABOUT THE MURDERS, GO TO 213. IF YOU WANT TO EXIT THE BUILDING, GO TO 62.

## 221.

## 222.

EACH POTION COSTS 3 GP AND GIVES YOU 1 HIT POINT OR 1 MAGIC POINT. YOU CHOOSE WHEN YOU USE IT.

AFTER YOU ARE DONE SHOPPING, RETURN TO THE ALLEY IN 82.

## 223.

YOU'VE JUST FOUND ONE OF THE MILITARY CAMPS OF DREADHORN COUNTY! DEEP IN THE FOREST OF WHITETHORN, THIS CAMP IS WHERE NEW RECRUITS TRAIN. TO TRY AND ENTER, GO TO 259. YOU CAN ALSO VISIT THE UNDERGROUND HOUSE IN 38, OR CONTINUE IN THE FOREST IN 63.

## 224.

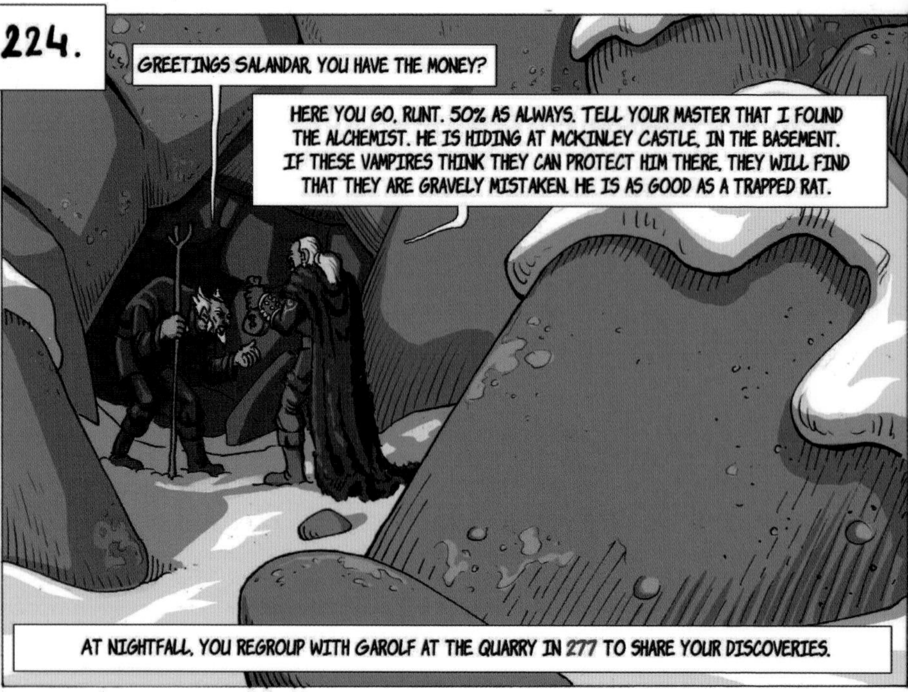

GREETINGS SALANDAR. YOU HAVE THE MONEY?

HERE YOU GO, RUNT. 50% AS ALWAYS. TELL YOUR MASTER THAT I FOUND THE ALCHEMIST. HE IS HIDING AT MCKINLEY CASTLE, IN THE BASEMENT. IF THESE VAMPIRES THINK THEY CAN PROTECT HIM THERE, THEY WILL FIND THAT THEY ARE GRAVELY MISTAKEN. HE IS AS GOOD AS A TRAPPED RAT.

AT NIGHTFALL, YOU REGROUP WITH GAROLF AT THE QUARRY IN 277 TO SHARE YOUR DISCOVERIES.

## 225.

EVEN WORSE, THESE BEASTS WILL THINK WE'RE RESPONS— WHAT'S THAT SOUND? WHO'S THERE?
CLAC!
YOU CANNOT HIDE ANYMORE! BOTH VAMPIRES HAVE SEEN YOU AND POUNCE ON YOU IN 90.

## 226.

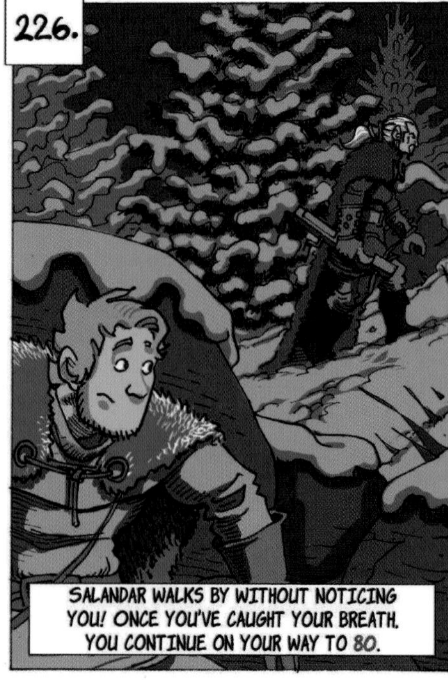
SALANDAR WALKS BY WITHOUT NOTICING YOU! ONCE YOU'VE CAUGHT YOUR BREATH, YOU CONTINUE ON YOUR WAY TO 80.

227.

YOU CAN ALWAYS RUN THEDOCRED, BUT I WILL CATCH YOU!

LUCKILY, THEDOCRED ESCAPED BEFORE OLDRAK COULD KILL HIM. HOWEVER, THERE'S NOT A MINUTE TO LOSE. THE LEADER OF THE PACK HAS ALMOST CAUGHT UP TO YOUR MASTER. HURRY UP AND FOLLOW THEM IN 317.

228.

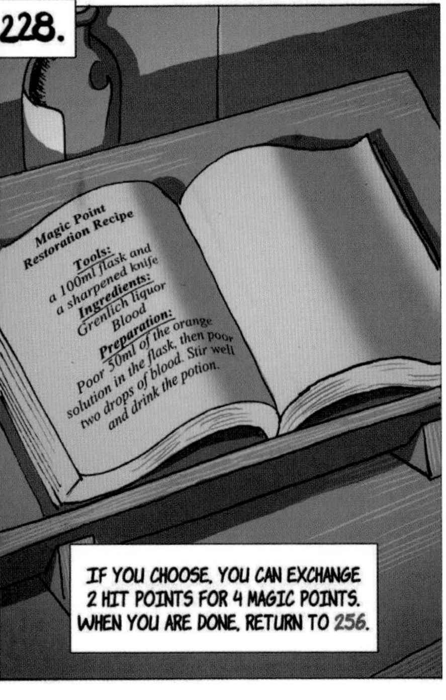
Magic Point
Restoration Recipe
Tools:
a 100ml flask and
a sharpened knife
Ingredients:
Grenlich liquor
Blood
Preparation:
Poor 50ml of the orange
solution in the flask, then poor
two drops of blood. Stir well
and drink the potion.
IF YOU CHOOSE, YOU CAN EXCHANGE 2 HIT POINTS FOR 4 MAGIC POINTS. WHEN YOU ARE DONE, RETURN TO 256.

229.

CRUD, YOU PICKED THE WRONG CHOICE! NOW HERE YOU ARE IN THE WATER! BUT DO NOT DESPAIR, YOU ARE NOT DEAD YET! CONTINUE TO SWIM TO 273.

230.
MOAT MONSTER
STRENGTH: 15
HIT POINTS: 24
LOOT: 1 POTION THAT GRANTS 4 MAGIC POINTS AND 2 HIT POINTS
XP EARNED: 5
XSSSS, WHO DAREZZZ SSSOJOURN IN MY WATERZZZ?
IF YOU DEFEAT THE CREATURE, YOU SWIM TO THE DRAWBRIDGE, CLAMBER UP, AND MAKE YOUR WAY TO 126. IF YOU RUN OUT OF HIT POINTS, YOU DIE AND MUST RESTART IN 1.

231.
113
303
5
60

232.
THIS STONE BED IS MUCH TOO UNCOMFORTABLE FOR YOU! GO BACK TO 142.

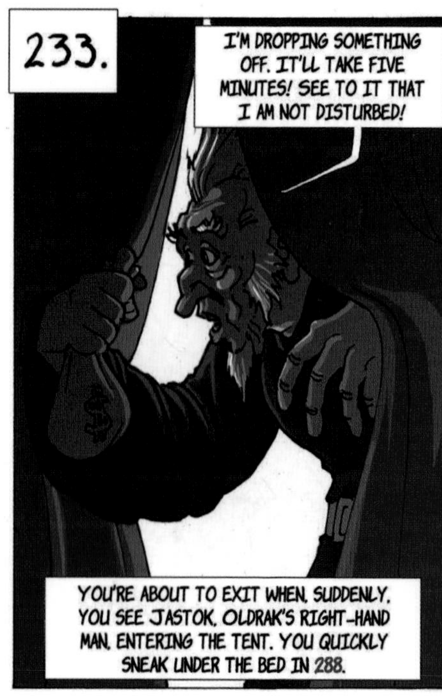
233.
I'M DROPPING SOMETHING OFF. IT'LL TAKE FIVE MINUTES! SEE TO IT THAT I AM NOT DISTURBED!
YOU'RE ABOUT TO EXIT WHEN, SUDDENLY, YOU SEE JASTOK, OLDRAK'S RIGHT-HAND MAN, ENTERING THE TENT. YOU QUICKLY SNEAK UNDER THE BED IN 288.

234.
HERE ENDS YOUR LIFE, WHELP!
WEREWOLF
STRENGTH: 20
HIT POINTS: 30
LOOT: A POTION THAT GRANTS 3 HIT POINTS
XP EARNED: 10
ONCE THE ROAD IS CLEAR, HEAD TO 267!

235.
THE SPIRAL IS THE SYMBOL OF OUR CLAN : CLAN MCKINLEY. EACH MEMBER HAS IT TATTOOED ON THEIR ARM.
IF YOU HAVE A SECOND QUESTION, RETURN TO 29, OTHERWISE GO TO 176.

236.

OH NO! YOU DIDN'T RECOGNIZE THE SIGN OF THE BLACK BROTHERHOOD ON THE PARCHMENT? SALANDAR RECOGNIZES YOU AND FIRES A BOLT STRAIGHT THROUGH YOUR HEART. YOU FALL TO THE GROUND AND LOSE CONSCIOUSNESS... FOREVER. RESTART IN PANEL 1.

## 237.

SO EORAS, WHERE TO NOW?

## 238.

SINCE THIS IS YOUR FIRST FULL MOON, WE CAN'T TAKE ANY CHANCES, AND YOU'LL NEED TO BE SHACKLED. WITH LUCK, EVERYTHING WILL BE FINE.

THERE'S A LUMP FORMING IN YOUR THROAT. EVEN THOUGH YOU ARE NOT ALONE AND THE FULL MOON IS HOURS AWAY, YOU ARE BECOMING INCREASINGLY CONCERNED ABOUT THE TRANSFORMATION. WHAT IF YOU DO NOT CHANGE BACK?
TIME PASSES, GO TO 30.

239.

NO NEED TO TELL ME ANYTHING. I KNOW YOU HAVE A JADE AMULET AND YOU WISH ME TO ENCHANT IT! AS YOU MUST KNOW, THAT IS NOT FREE. YOU MUST SACRIFICE 1 STRENGTH OR 1 DEFENSE FOR IT. IF YOU AGREE, MEET ME IN 31. OTHERWISE, LEAVE IN 321!

THERE IS A THIRD OPTION : THREATEN THE SEER IN 49, AT YOUR PERIL...

240.

153

AND ONE LESS!

6

TO RETURN TO THE HALLWAY, GO BACK TO 143.

# 241.

PASSWORD?!

IF YOU KNOW THE PASSWORD, OR ARE WEARING A MORGUE EMPLOYEE UNIFORM, YOU MAY GO TO 128. OTHERWISE, THE MAN LETS YOU IN FOR 30 GP. IF YOU'RE WILLING TO GET YOUR HANDS DIRTY, YOU CAN WAIT FOR ANOTHER EMPLOYEE TO EXIT AND FOLLOW HIM IN 258. TO RETURN TO THE STREET, GO TO 62.

# 242.

HUZZAH! YOU'VE GOT SALANDAR ON THE RUN! WITH THOSE HOUNDS ON HIS TRAIL, YOU WON'T SEE HIM ANYTIME SOON! YOU GAIN 3 XP. FINALLY, CONTINUE YOUR ADVENTURE IN 32.

243.

BE CAREFUL. THE SOLDIERS PERCHED ON THE RAMPARTS ARE CONTINUALLY FIRING AND YOU LOSE 1 HIT POINT. TAKE COVER BEHIND THE SIEGE TOWER IN 248 OR JOIN THE BATTERING RAM IN 313 TO ATTEMPT TO OPEN THE LARGE WOODEN DOOR.

244.

PSSST, FRIEND. I'VE GOT SOME MERCHANDISE YOU MAY BE INTERESTED IN. IF YOU'RE LOOKING FOR A JADE AMULET, COME TO 217.

IF YOU'RE NOT INTERESTED, GO BACK TO 254.

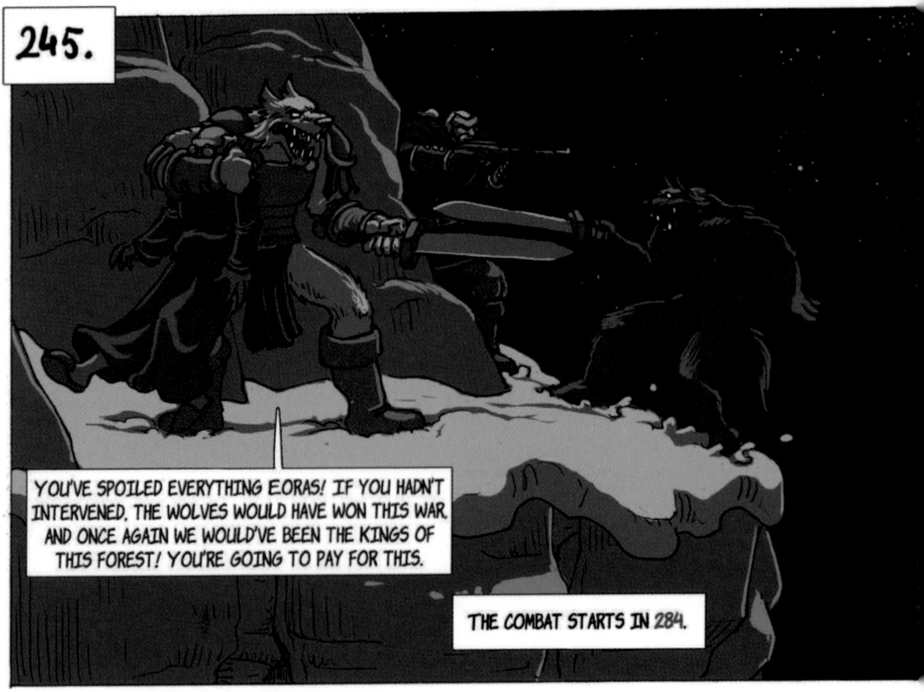

245.

YOU'VE SPOILED EVERYTHING EORAS! IF YOU HADN'T INTERVENED, THE WOLVES WOULD HAVE WON THIS WAR AND ONCE AGAIN WE WOULD'VE BEEN THE KINGS OF THIS FOREST! YOU'RE GOING TO PAY FOR THIS.

THE COMBAT STARTS IN 284.

246.
AMONG THE MESS, YOU FIND A FLASK THAT GIVES YOU 2 MAGIC POINTS. GO BACK TO 303.

247.
THE STREAM HAS CARRIED YOU TOWARDS THE BRIDGE. TAKE YOUR BREATH AND GO BACK TO 199.

248.
EORAS! QUICKLY! FIND A WAY TO MOVE THE SIEGE ENGINE!
3
35
THE SIEGE ENGINE ALLOWS YOU TO HIDE AND AVOID THE SALVO OF ARROWS THAT COULD HAVE KILLED YOU IN MERE SECONDS. SADLY, THE WHEELS OF THE SIEGE ENGINE ARE STUCK IN THE MUD. YOU MUST QUICKLY FIND A WAY TO FREE IT...
249.
CONGRATULATIONS! YOU'VE SURVIVED YOUR FIRST TRANSFORMATION! DON'T FORGET THAT IF YOU FIND A JADE AMULET AND HAVE IT ENCHANTED, YOU WILL BE ABLE TO TRANSFORM WHENEVER YOU WANT. IF YOU DO NOT FIND ONE, YOU CAN UNLOCK THE SPELL "FULL MOON" WITH ENOUGH EXPERIENCE.
YOU WILL NEED TO TRANSFORM TO DEFEAT SOME ENEMIES. AT THE END OF COMBAT, YOU WILL DECIDE WHETHER YOU WISH TO RETURN TO YOUR HUMAN FORM OR STAY A WEREWOLF, IN WHICH CASE, WATCH WHERE YOU DECIDE TO WANDER! THE BLACK BROTHERHOOD, A GROUP OF WEREWOLF HUNTERS, IS LURKING IN TOWN. IF THEY FIND AN ANIMAL, THEY WILL NOT HESITATE TO KILL IT! YOU CAN RECOGNIZE THEM BY THEIR INSIGNIA: A HALF-MOON.
STILL DAZED BY THE NIGHT, YOU GRAB THE SKULL KEY OFFERED BY MADAM VARG AND HEAD TOWARDS THE UPPER LEVEL. THANKING YOUR HOSTS, YOU HEAD BACK TO THE FOREST IN 179.

## 250.

HEY, I RECOGNIZE YOU! YOU SPENT LAST NIGHT AT OUR PLACE! SORRY, I WOULD'VE LIKED TO INTRODUCE MY FRIENDS UNDER BETTER CIRCUMSTANCES, BUT MEMBERS OF THE PACK HAVE BEEN MYSTERIOUSLY DISAPPEARING.

IF YOU WISH TO LEARN MORE ABOUT THIS SUBJECT, JOIN GAROLF'S DAUGHTER IN 58. OTHERWISE, YOU CAN GO BACK TO 167.

## 251.

JUST A LITTLE FURTHER! ONE MORE PULL TO REACH THE SUMMIT IN 267.

252.
223

253.
THE RAMPART BELONGS TO US, BROTHERS! CHARGE THE ENEMY!
YOU ARE FINALLY CLOSE TO YOUR GOAL OF ENTERING THE CASTLE! GO TO 89 TO CONTINUE THE BATTLE.

254.

18

46

244

TO VISIT ANOTHER DISTRICT, GO TO 180!

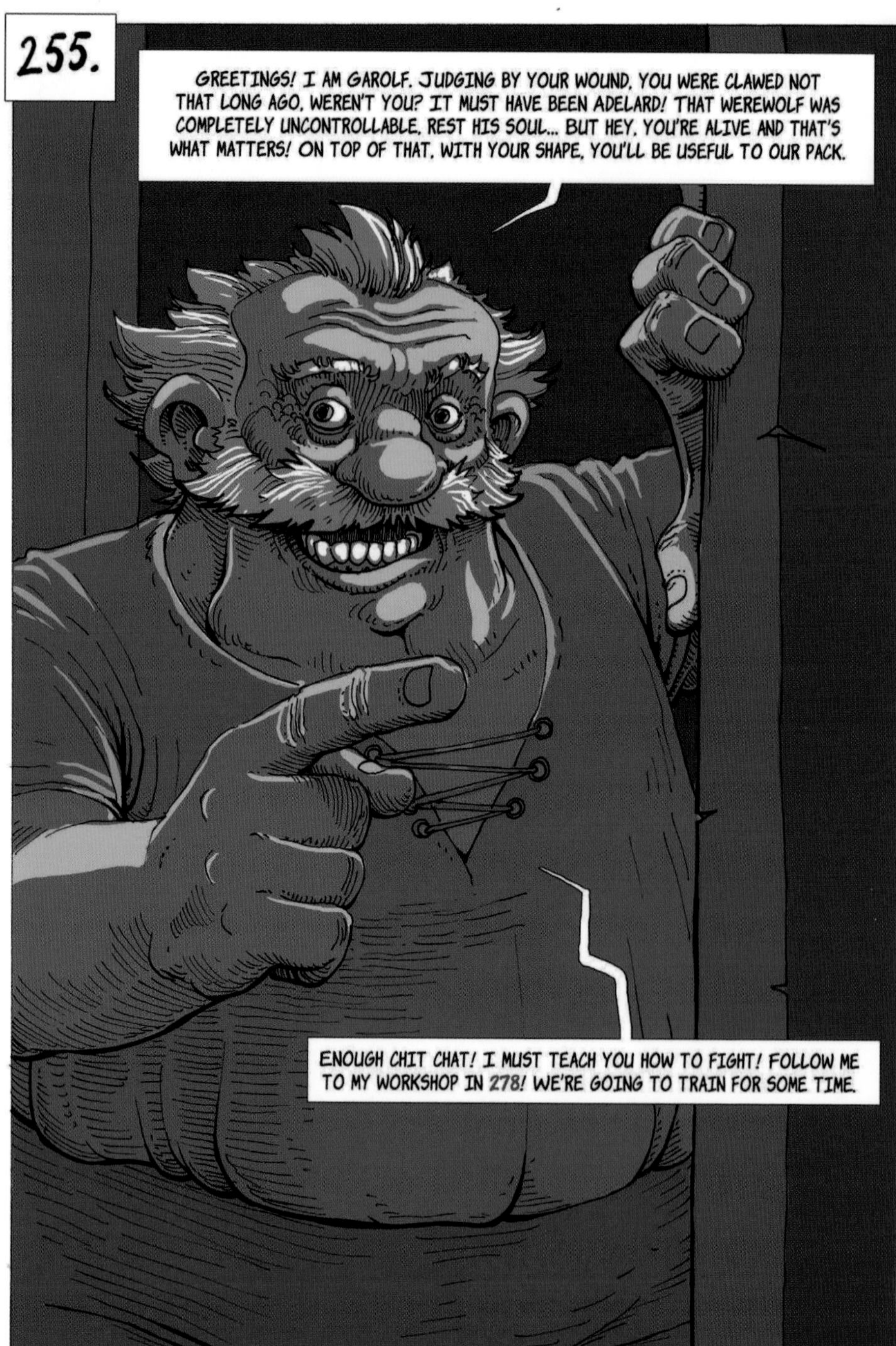
255.
GREETINGS! I AM GAROLF. JUDGING BY YOUR WOUND, YOU WERE CLAWED NOT THAT LONG AGO, WEREN'T YOU? IT MUST HAVE BEEN ADELARD! THAT WEREWOLF WAS COMPLETELY UNCONTROLLABLE. REST HIS SOUL... BUT HEY, YOU'RE ALIVE AND THAT'S WHAT MATTERS! ON TOP OF THAT, WITH YOUR SHAPE, YOU'LL BE USEFUL TO OUR PACK.
ENOUGH CHIT CHAT! I MUST TEACH YOU HOW TO FIGHT! FOLLOW ME TO MY WORKSHOP IN 278! WE'RE GOING TO TRAIN FOR SOME TIME.

## 256.

228

133

TO RETURN TO THE LABORATORY ENTRANCE, GO TO 200.

## 257.

GREETINGS! ARE YOU INTERESTED IN SOME OF MY JEWELRY? THE RINGS GRANT YOU 1 HIT POINT AFTER EACH COMBAT, WHILE THE AMULET GRANTS YOU 2 MAGIC POINTS. AS FOR THE JADE AMULET, IT'S RATHER SPECIAL. ONCE ENCHANTED, IT ALLOWS WEREWOLVES TO TRANSFORM ON ANY NIGHT. AT LEAST, THAT'S WHAT THEY SAY. I'M NOT A HORRIBLE *LOUP GAROU*, SO I DON'T KNOW IF IT REALLY WORKS.

JADE AMULET: 25 GP
RINGS: 15 GP
AMULET: 15 GP

ONCE YOU'RE DONE SHOPPING, GO BACK TO 82.

## 258.

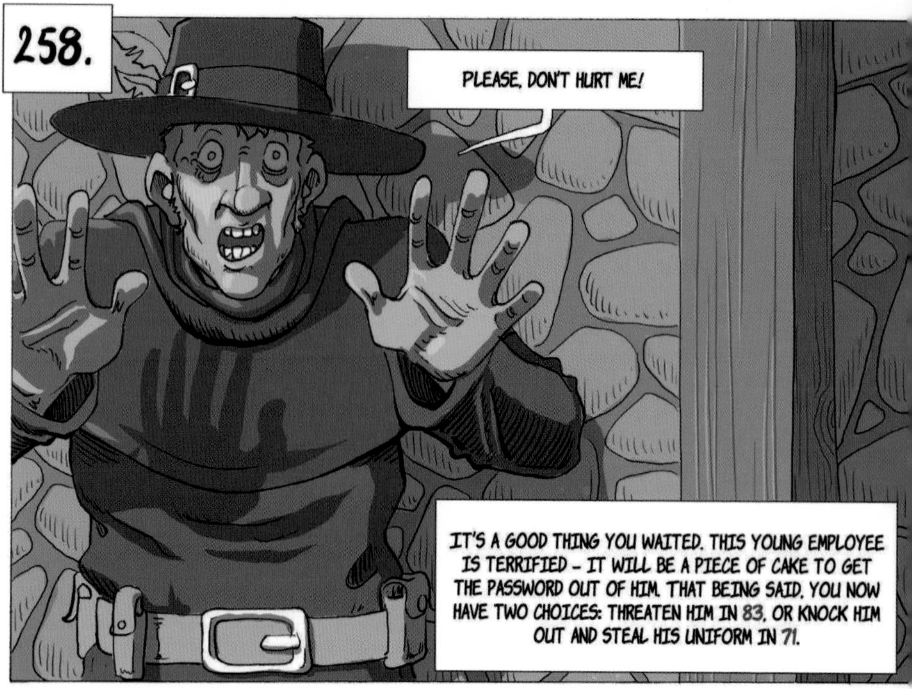

PLEASE, DON'T HURT ME!

IT'S A GOOD THING YOU WAITED. THIS YOUNG EMPLOYEE IS TERRIFIED – IT WILL BE A PIECE OF CAKE TO GET THE PASSWORD OUT OF HIM. THAT BEING SAID, YOU NOW HAVE TWO CHOICES: THREATEN HIM IN 83, OR KNOCK HIM OUT AND STEAL HIS UNIFORM IN 71.

## 259.

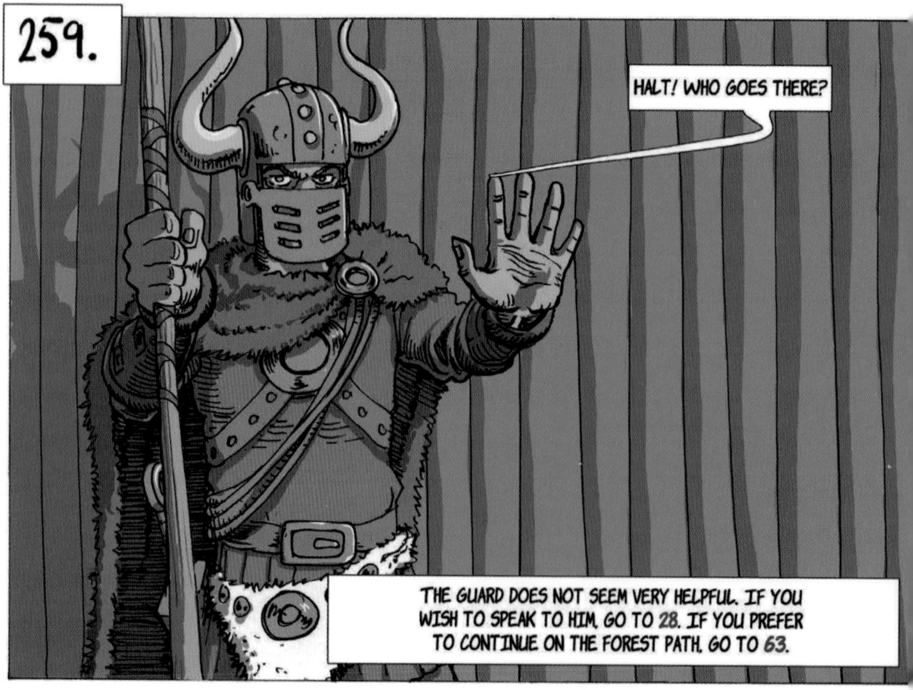

HALT! WHO GOES THERE?

THE GUARD DOES NOT SEEM VERY HELPFUL. IF YOU WISH TO SPEAK TO HIM, GO TO 28. IF YOU PREFER TO CONTINUE ON THE FOREST PATH, GO TO 63.

260.
Vampire
Ogre
Liche
Loup Garou
STRANGE... WHY WAS YOUR MASTER READING THIS GRIMOIRE? WAS HE RESEARCHING THESE CREATURES DURING YOUR ABSENCE? IT'S UP TO YOU TO SOLVE THIS MYSTERY! GO BACK TO THE LABORATORY ENTRANCE IN 169.

261.
KEEP FOLLOWING JASTOK IN 274.

262.
203
47

263.
THIS SNAKE LOOKS RATHER DOCILE. HE WOULD MAKE A GOOD COMPANION. IF YOU ALREADY HAVE A COMPANION, YOU MUST NOW CHOOSE WHICH TO KEEP!
SNAKE
BONUS: IF YOU OBTAIN A 2 YOU MAY RESPIN, BUT YOU WILL HAVE TO ACCEPT THE SECOND SPIN, EVEN IF IT'S WORSE.
GO BACK TO 78!

## 264.

YOUR ADVENTURE ENDS HERE, WOLF!

VAMPIRE

STRENGTH: 12
HIT POINTS: 21
LOOT: 1 POTION THAT GRANTS 2 HIT POINTS
XP EARNED: 7

ONCE YOU'VE DEFEATED THIS VAMPIRE, CHOOSE YOUR PATH! RUSH TO THE HEART OF THE BATTLE IN 103, OR HEAD TOWARDS THE CATAPULTS IN 170.

## 265.

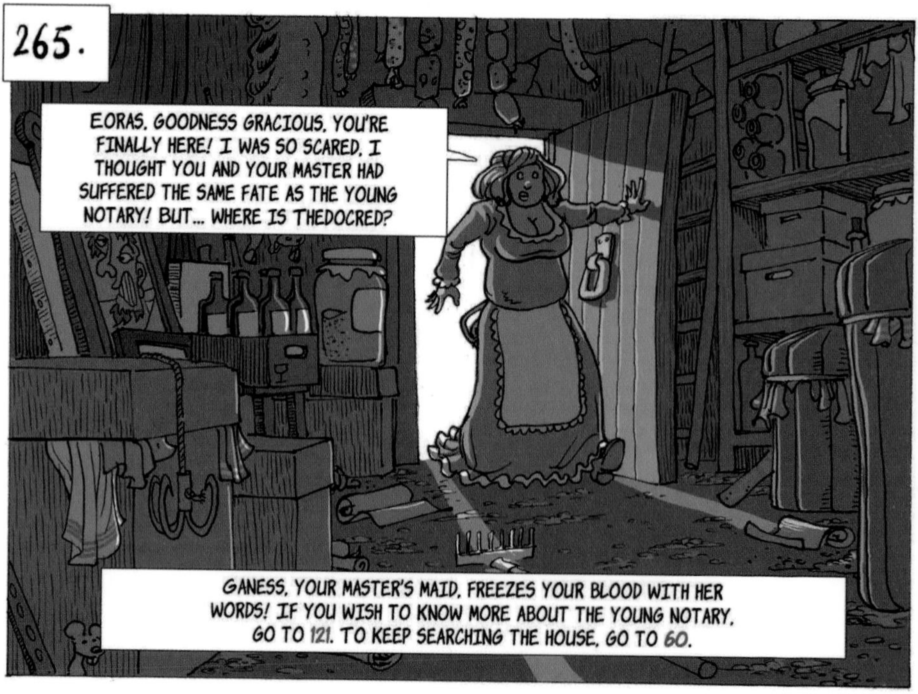

EORAS, GOODNESS GRACIOUS, YOU'RE FINALLY HERE! I WAS SO SCARED, I THOUGHT YOU AND YOUR MASTER HAD SUFFERED THE SAME FATE AS THE YOUNG NOTARY! BUT... WHERE IS THEDOCRED?

GANESS, YOUR MASTER'S MAID, FREEZES YOUR BLOOD WITH HER WORDS! IF YOU WISH TO KNOW MORE ABOUT THE YOUNG NOTARY, GO TO 121. TO KEEP SEARCHING THE HOUSE, GO TO 60.

## 266.

WELCOME AT MY SUPERNATURAL SHOP! IF YER INTERESTED MY WARES, LET ME KNOW!

- AMULET OF THE DAMNED (+2 MAGIC POINTS AT THE END OF COMBAT): 30 GP
- TAROT DECK: 5 GP
- SCHOLAR'S BAG (15 SLOTS): 25 GP
- SNAKE WINE (+5 HIT POINTS): 15 GP
- JADE AMULET: 25 GP
- ENCHANTED APPLES/PEARS (+1 HIT POINT): 3 GP
- CORRUPTED CINNAMON STICK (+1 MAGIC POINT): 3 GP

AFTER CONCLUDING YOUR PURCHASES, HEAD BACK ON THE TRAIL IN 204!

## 267.

YOU'VE JUST REACHED THE TOP OF THE CLIFF WHEN A SHARP BLADE BRUSHES AGAINST YOUR THROAT.

YOUR HEART BEATS WILDLY AS YOU USE YOUR NEWFOUND POWERS. YOU GET OUT OF OLDRAK'S STRANGLEHOLD, PUNCH HIM IN THE RIBS, AND PICK UP YOUR WEAPON. GO TO 245.

## 268.

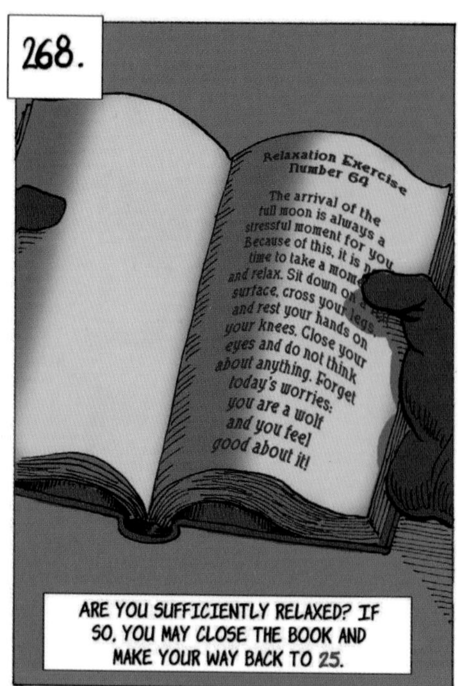
Relaxation Exercise
Number 64
The arrival of the
full moon is always a
stressful moment for you
Because of this, it is
time to take a
and relax. Sit down on
surface, cross your legs
and rest your hands on
your knees. Close your
eyes and do not think
about anything. Forget
today's worries:
you are a wolf
and you feel
good about it!
ARE YOU SUFFICIENTLY RELAXED? IF SO, YOU MAY CLOSE THE BOOK AND MAKE YOUR WAY BACK TO 25.

## 269.

302

## 270.

WHAT HAPPENED TO ME?! I WAS WITH OLDRAK WHEN, ALL OF A SUDDEN, I GOT HIT ON THE HEAD...

YOU HELP GAROLF STAND UP AND ASK HIM WHERE OLDRAK IS. YOUR FRIEND POINTS TO THE DOOR IN FRONT OF YOU. ALAS, IT'S LOCKED AND TWO KEYS ARE REQUIRED TO OPEN IT. IF YOU HAVE FOUND BOTH KEYS IN THIS FORTRESS, GO TO 307. OTHERWISE, GO BACK TO 122 TO LOOK FOR THEM!

271.
OH NO! IN YOUR HASTE, YOU FOLLOWED THE WRONG PERSON. YOU MAY BE ABLE TO CATCH UP TO THE EMPLOYEE YOU WERE SHADOWING BY HEADING TOWARD THE MORGUE. RUN TO 16.

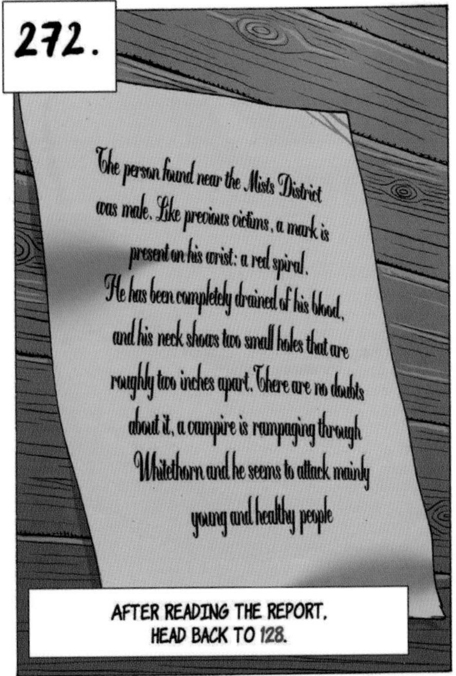
272.
The person found near the Mists District was male. Like previous victims, a mark is present on his wrist: a red spiral. He has been completely drained of his blood, and his neck shows two small holes that are roughly two inches apart. There are no doubts about it, a vampire is rampaging through Whitethorn and he seems to attack mainly young and healthy people
AFTER READING THE REPORT, HEAD BACK TO 128.

273.
SALANDAR IS ABOUT TO FIRE HIS BOLTS. YOU MUST CHOOSE QUICKLY BEFORE YOU GET HIT! CONTINUE SWIMMING TO REACH THE OTHER SHORE IN 312, OR TRY TO SURVIVE BY GOING UNDERWATER IN 87.

274.
YOU CAN FOLLOW OLDRAK'S RIGHT-HAND MAN IN 93, OR HIDE BEHIND A ROCK TO SPY ON HIM IN 224.

# 275.

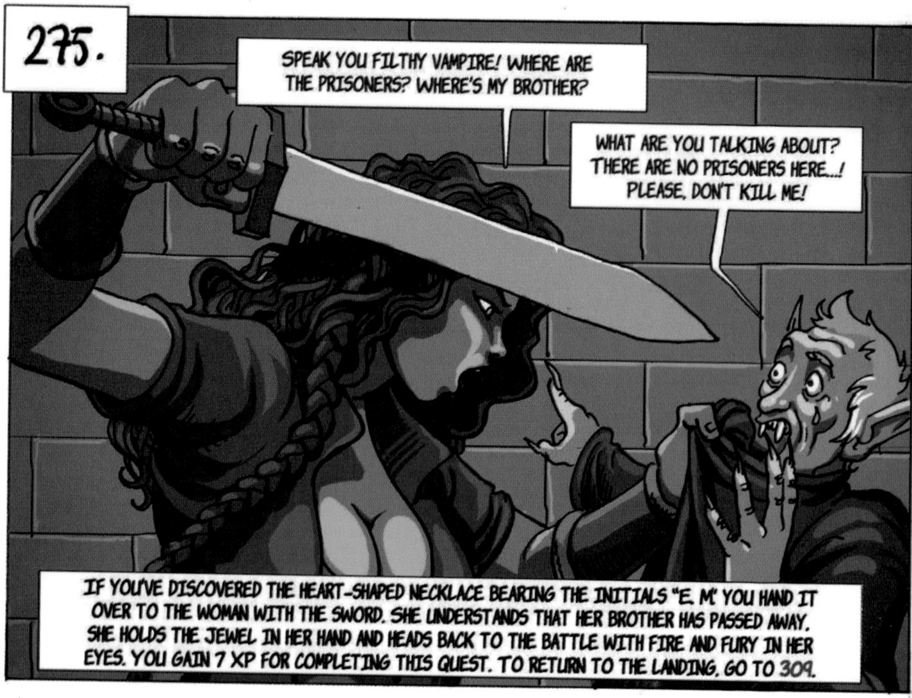

SPEAK YOU FILTHY VAMPIRE! WHERE ARE THE PRISONERS? WHERE'S MY BROTHER?

WHAT ARE YOU TALKING ABOUT? THERE ARE NO PRISONERS HERE...! PLEASE, DON'T KILL ME!

IF YOU'VE DISCOVERED THE HEART-SHAPED NECKLACE BEARING THE INITIALS "E. M." YOU HAND IT OVER TO THE WOMAN WITH THE SWORD. SHE UNDERSTANDS THAT HER BROTHER HAS PASSED AWAY. SHE HOLDS THE JEWEL IN HER HAND AND HEADS BACK TO THE BATTLE WITH FIRE AND FURY IN HER EYES. YOU GAIN 7 XP FOR COMPLETING THIS QUEST. TO RETURN TO THE LANDING, GO TO 309.

# 276.

63

308

2

IF THIS IS YOUR FIRST TIME HERE, YOU FEEL SOMEONE TAPPING ON YOUR SHOULDER. YOU TURN AROUND IN 114.

## 277.

IF WHAT WE'VE DISCOVERED SO FAR IS TRUE, THEN IT'S A CATASTROPHE... I...

YOUR CONVERSATION IS CUT SHORT BY THE SOUND OF A HUNTING HORN! YOUR HEART IS POUNDING. WITH YOUR RECENT DISCOVERIES, YOU HAVE NO DESIRE TO PARTICIPATE IN THIS BATTLE. FROM WHAT YOU'VE FOUND, IT IS OBVIOUS THAT THE VAMPIRES ARE NOT RESPONSIBLE FOR THE WEREWOLF DISAPPEARANCES! GO TO 198.

## 278.

ONCE YOU GET OUTTA HERE, YOU'LL MOST LIKELY CROSS PATH WITH MANY DANGEROUS AND VILE CREATURES.

BUT I'M NOT WORRIED ABOUT YOU. YOU LOOK HARDY ENOUGH. I KNOW YOU'LL MAKE IT!

IT IS NOW TIME TO TEST YOUR METTLE IN COMBAT! ONWARD TO PANEL 45.

279.

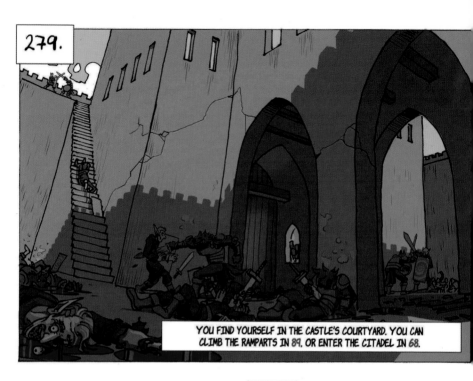

YOU FIND YOURSELF IN THE CASTLE'S COURTYARD. YOU CAN CLIMB THE RAMPARTS IN 89, OR ENTER THE CITADEL IN 68.

280.
EASY: EACH DOMINO HAD ITS INVERTED TWIN, EXCEPT FOR ONE, 5/4!
YER RIGHT FÆGAL! THE ANSWER WAS 4/5!
IF YOUR ANSWER WAS IN FACT 4/5, YOU GET THE FISHING HOOK, 2 XP FOR SOLVING THE RIDDLE, AND CAN GO FISHING IN 298! IF YOU DID NOT FIND THE RIGHT ANSWER, GO BACK TO 22. THIS RIDDLE IS NO LONGER AVAILABLE.

281.
STAY HERE? MOST CERTAINLY NOT! EVEN IF I HAVE MY DOUBTS REGARDING OLDRAK'S TRUE MOTIVATIONS, I HAVE TO DO ALL I CAN TO FIND MY BROTHER! HE DISAPPEARED TWO DAYS AGO.
YOU CAN RETRACE YOUR STEPS IN 104, ASK HER TO SHARPEN YOUR BLADE IN 115, OR POSE MORE QUESTIONS ABOUT OLDRAK IN 182.

282.

I WOULD'VE LOVED TO GO OUT AND WALK AROUND WITH YOU, BUT MY PARENTS GROUNDED ME. APPARENTLY, YOU CAN'T BURN YOUR SISTER'S HAIR.
IF YOU'RE INTERESTED IN MY BOOK, YOU CAN READ IT!
IF YOU WISH TO READ JAMIE'S BOOK, GO TO 44. OTHERWISE, GO BACK TO 209!


283.

THE MAN I BURIED WAS UNLIKE ANY OTHER. DRAINED OF HIS BLOOD, THERE WAS A STRANGE MARK ON HIS SKIN: A RED SPIRAL! EVEN STRANGER, TODAY, HIS BODY DISAPPEARED FROM HIS TOMB!
TO RETURN TO THE TEMPLE HALL, GO TO 46.

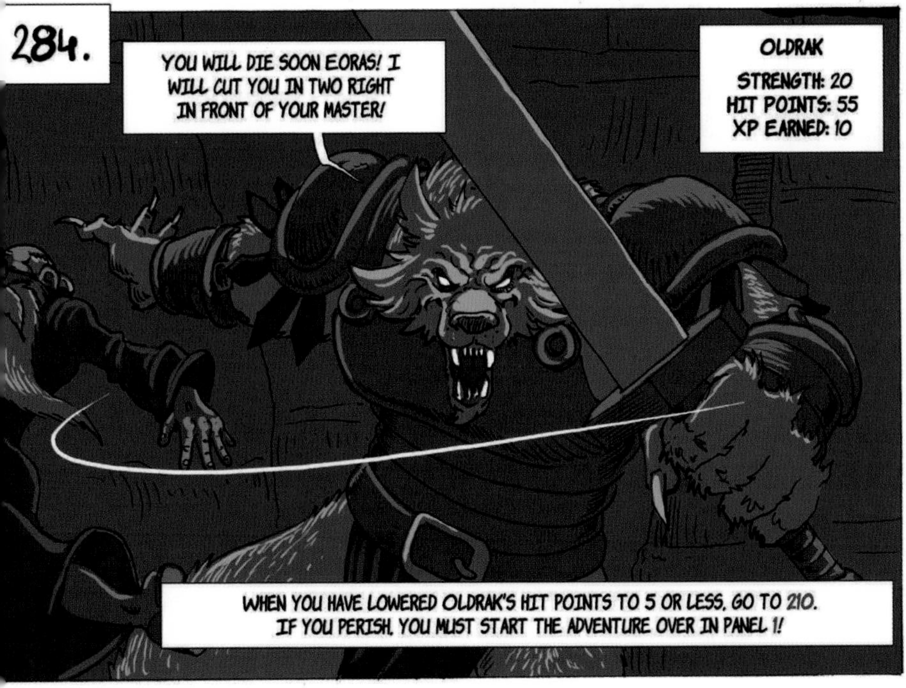

284.

YOU WILL DIE SOON EORAS! I WILL CUT YOU IN TWO RIGHT IN FRONT OF YOUR MASTER!

**OLDRAK**

STRENGTH: 20
HIT POINTS: 55
XP EARNED: 10

WHEN YOU HAVE LOWERED OLDRAK'S HIT POINTS TO 5 OR LESS, GO TO 210.
IF YOU PERISH, YOU MUST START THE ADVENTURE OVER IN PANEL 1!

285.
GET THE BEST ARMOR IN THE COUNTRY RIGHT HERE!
EXCEPTIONAL MEAT FOR YOU LADIES AND GENTLEMEN!
FRESHEST SALMON IN TOWN!
IF FATHER BARNABY THE BUTCHER'S STALL INTERESTS YOU, YOU CAN PAY HIM A VISIT IN 41.
YOU CAN ALSO STROLL TOWARDS THE ARMORER IN 100, OR RETRACE YOUR STEPS TO 318.

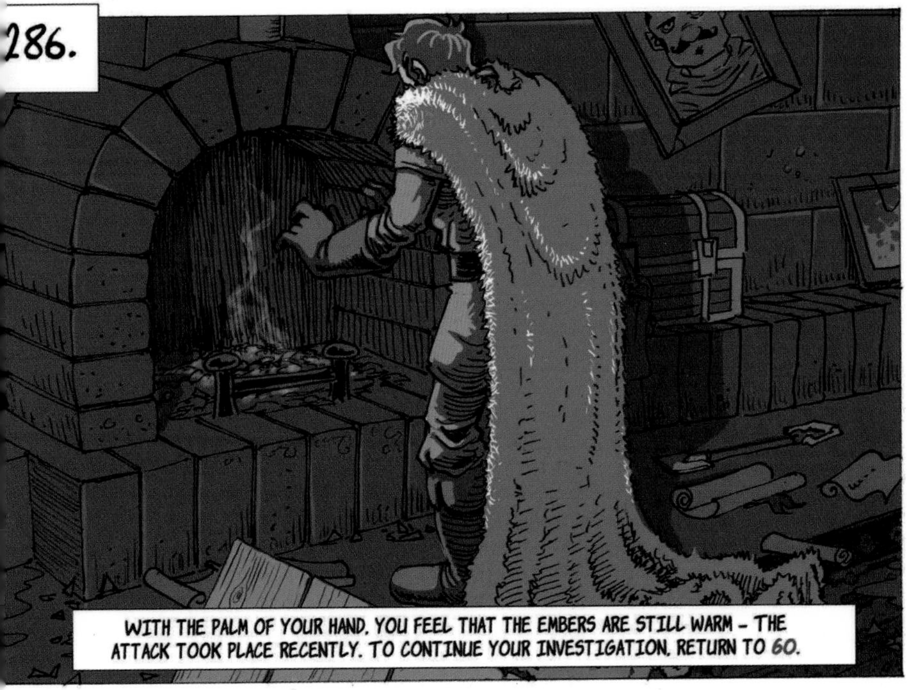

## 286.

WITH THE PALM OF YOUR HAND, YOU FEEL THAT THE EMBERS ARE STILL WARM – THE ATTACK TOOK PLACE RECENTLY. TO CONTINUE YOUR INVESTIGATION, RETURN TO 60.

## 287.

A NEW CHOICE IS BEFORE YOU: WILL YOU RUSH TO THE RESCUE OF THIS POOR WOMAN IN 175 OR CONTINUE ON YOUR WAY IN 65 IN THE HOPES THAT THIS AWFUL BANDIT DOES NOT SEE YOU?

## 288.

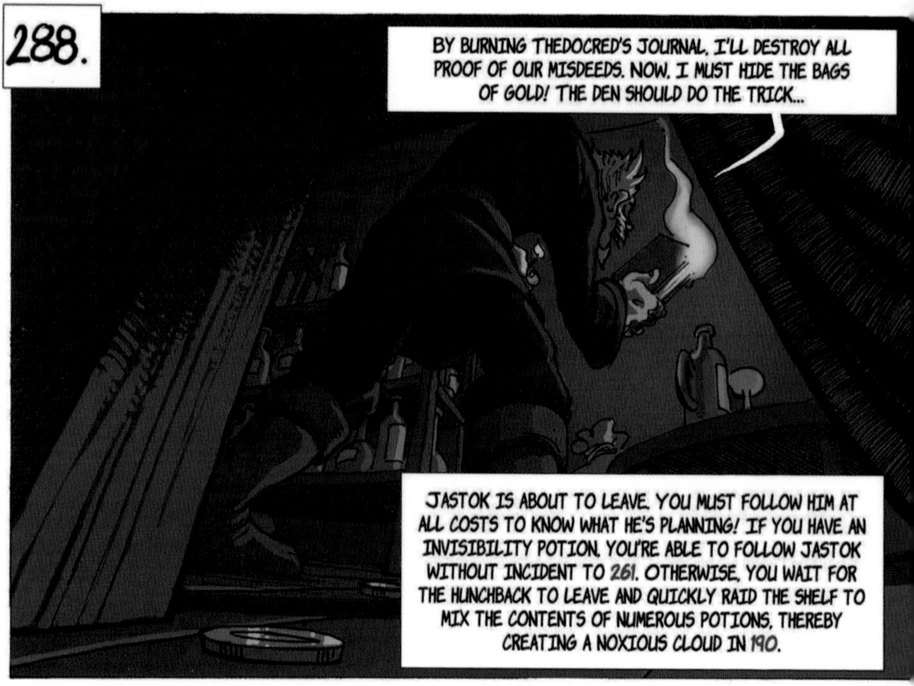

BY BURNING THEDOCRED'S JOURNAL, I'LL DESTROY ALL PROOF OF OUR MISDEEDS. NOW, I MUST HIDE THE BAGS OF GOLD! THE DEN SHOULD DO THE TRICK...

JASTOK IS ABOUT TO LEAVE. YOU MUST FOLLOW HIM AT ALL COSTS TO KNOW WHAT HE'S PLANNING! IF YOU HAVE AN INVISIBILITY POTION, YOU'RE ABLE TO FOLLOW JASTOK WITHOUT INCIDENT TO 261. OTHERWISE, YOU WAIT FOR THE HUNCHBACK TO LEAVE AND QUICKLY RAID THE SHELF TO MIX THE CONTENTS OF NUMEROUS POTIONS, THEREBY CREATING A NOXIOUS CLOUD IN 190.

## 289.

17

226

59

290.
IMPALED BY AN ARROW, THIS VAMPIRE FALLS DEAD BEFORE HE COULD EVEN RAISE HIS SWORD. YOU TAKE OFF OF HIM A MAGIC POTION THAT GIVES 2 MAGIC POINTS. CONTINUE TO 135.

291.
YOUR ADVENTURE ENDS HERE!
THE BOLT GOES STRAIGHT THROUGH YOUR HEART. START OVER IN PANEL 1.

292.
THIS ROCK ALMOST MADE YOU FALL ALL THE WAY DOWN, BUT YOU GRAB ONTO THE CLIFF AT THE LAST MOMENT AND PULL YOURSELF UP IN 267. HOWEVER, YOU'VE BEEN HURT AND LOSE 1 HIT POINT.

293.

## 294.

85

201

HERE IS THE RED DISTRICT! IT IS UP TO YOU TO DECIDE WHERE YOU WILL GO: THE FORGE OR THE MONASTERY. TO VISIT ANOTHER DISTRICT, CONSULT THE MAP IN 180.

## 295.

DUKE MCKINLEY HAS ENTRUSTED ME WITH ONE OF HIS KEYS! IT OPENS THE BASEMENT DOOR, BUT IF YOU WANT IT, YOU MUST SOLVE THIS RIDDLE...

...EACH HAS HIS OWN,
THAT NONE MAY COPY,
FOR IMITATING IT
MAY LOCK YOU UP.
FAMOUS AND OFFICIAL,
IT IS OFTEN REQUESTED,
AND YET, A SIMPLE
CROSS MAY REPLACE IT.

GO TO 57.

296.

AFTER A 30-FOOT FALL, YOU COME BACK TO YOUR SENSES AND GET BACK UP IN 3. YOU DO LOSE 1 HIT POINT, HOWEVER.

297.

79

218

201

298.
GOODNESS, NOW THAT'S A FISH!
YOU CAN PUT THIS FISH IN YOUR BAG AND EAT IT AT ANY TIME TO REGAIN 2 HIT POINTS.
THEN RETURN TO 22.

299.
LOYAL DOG
BONUS: +1 STRENGTH AND +2 DEFENSE
WHEW, ONLY A DOG! YOU FREE THE POOR ANIMAL WHO CAN, IF YOU SO DESIRE, BECOME YOUR COMPANION (IF YOU ALREADY HAVE ONE, YOU MUST CHOOSE AND MAY KEEP ONLY ONE).
THEN RETURN TO 55.

300.

42

155

67

301.
AFTER WALKING THROUGH THE FOREST FOR A GOOD HOUR, YOU HAVE FINALLY REACHED THE WEREWOLVES' CAMP.
A FEW HOURS AGO, THE SIMPLE THOUGHT OF GOING BACK TO TOWN WAS ENOUGH TO MAKE YOU HAPPY. THIS BRIEF MEMORY, HOWEVER, HAS LEFT YOU WITH DEEP ANGUISH: THEDOCRED HAS MYSTERIOUSLY DISAPPEARED AND STILL NO TRACE OF HIM! ALL THAT YOU KNOW, IS THAT A CLAN OF VAMPIRES CALLED THE MCKINLEY CLAN HAS RECRUITED MANY TOWNSFOLK.
FROM WHAT YOU OVERHEARD IN THE OLD LIBRARY, THEY AREN'T RESPONSIBLE FOR THE WEREWOLF DISAPPEARANCES, BUT IF THAT IS TRUE THEN WHO IS RESPONSIBLE? WHO DO THE VAMPIRES FEAR SO MUCH THAT THEY'D RAISE SUCH AN ARMY? ARE THEY LINKED TO THEDOCRED'S DISAPPEARANCE? IS YOUR MENTOR STILL ALIVE?
THOSE ARE ONLY A FEW OF THE QUESTIONS TO WHICH YOU MUST FIND THE ANSWER...
HERE'S THE PACK! I WILL INTRODUCE YOU TO OLDRAK, OUR LEADER. HE'S SOMEWHAT BOORISH, BUT I'M CERTAIN HE'LL ACCEPT YOU AMONG US!
IT'S A GOOD THING THAT GAROLF IS HERE TO HELP YOU. WITH A BIT OF LUCK, OLDRAK WILL ALSO HAVE NEW TRACKS FOR YOU TO FOLLOW. GO MEET HIM IN 27.

# 302.

YOUR SMALL BOAT IS SWAYING DANGEROUSLY! IMMEDIATELY SPIN YOUR DISK TO LEARN YOUR FATE. IF YOUR RESULT IS 1-2-3, GO TO 160. IF YOU OBTAINED 4-5-6, MAKE YOUR WAY TO 24.

# 303.

164

246

AH, YOUR ROOM! YOU REMEMBER HIDING A FEW POTIONS UNDER YOUR BED...

TO RETURN TO THE HALLWAY, GO TO 231.

304.

264

159

305.
CAN'T YOU READ? THE SIGNPOST YOU PASSED CLEARLY SAID "QUICKSAND!" IN A LITTLE OVER 30 SECONDS. YOUR BODY IS COMPLETELY BOGGED DOWN. YOUR ADVENTURE ENDS HERE. HEAD TO PANEL 1 TO START OVER AT THE VERY BEGINNING!

306.
256
215
IF YOU DO NOT WISH TO SPEND MORE TIME THAN YOU NEED TO IN THIS HALLWAY, GO BACK TO THE RECEPTION AREA IN 54.

## 307.

WORRIED ABOUT MISTER VINUS, YOU DECIDE TO TELL GAROLF EVERYTHING ABOUT OLDRAK'S BETRAYAL AND THE VAMPIRES' INNOCENCE.

GO FIND THEDOCRED! MEANWHILE, I'LL LOOK FOR A SOLUTION TO HELP MISTER VINUS AND END THIS BATTLE!

DESCEND INTO THE BASEMENT TO CHASE OLDRAK IN 55.

## 308.

163

276

309.

112

143

202

275

68

310.
MUTANT LIZARD
STRENGTH: 6
HIT POINTS: 16
LOOT: 5 GP
XP EARNED: 4
SMELLS LIKE FRESH MEAT! YUMMY!
THIS LIZARD WANTS TO MAKE YOU ITS MEAL. KILL IT AND GO BACK TO 142!

311.
WANTED!
YELLOW-FOOT
LEADER OF THE ASSASSINS' GUILD
DEAD OR ALIVE 20 GOLD PIECES
YOU'RE REMINDED OF A MEMORY! YOU RECOGNIZE THIS BRUTE: WHEN YOU WERE YOUNGER, HE BEAT YOU UP AND STOLE ALL OF YOUR GOLD PIECES. IT IS NOW TIME TO GET YOUR REVENGE. RETURN TO THE STREET IN 206 TO START LOOKING FOR HIM.

# 312.

CONGRATULATIONS, YOU'VE REACHED THE OTHER SIDE! BUT FORGET ABOUT RESTING ON YOUR LAURELS, AS SALANDAR IS STILL PURSUING YOU! GO TO 262!

# 313.

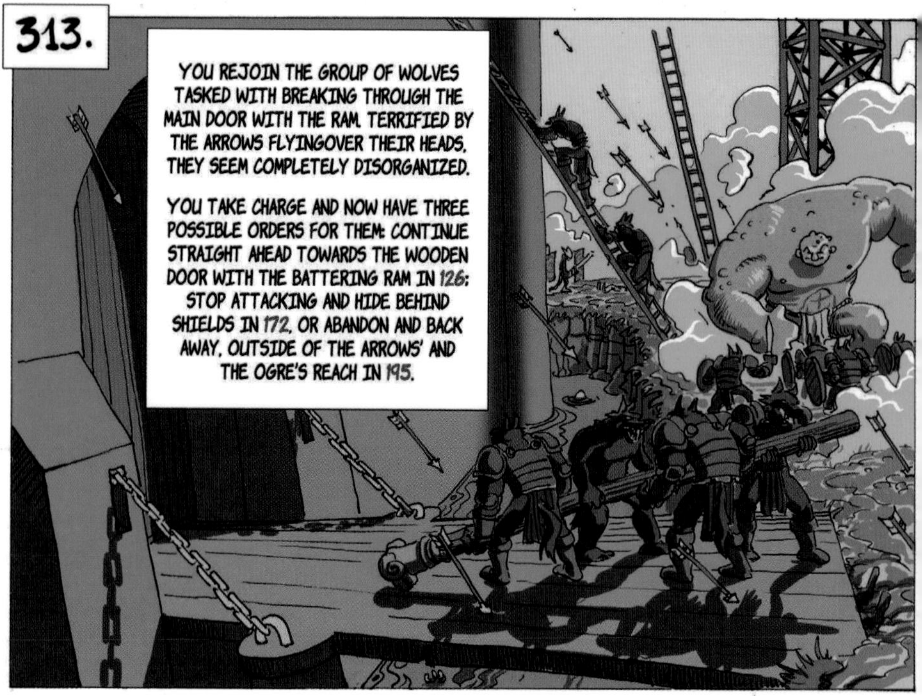

YOU REJOIN THE GROUP OF WOLVES TASKED WITH BREAKING THROUGH THE MAIN DOOR WITH THE RAM. TERRIFIED BY THE ARROWS FLYINGOVER THEIR HEADS, THEY SEEM COMPLETELY DISORGANIZED.

YOU TAKE CHARGE AND NOW HAVE THREE POSSIBLE ORDERS FOR THEM: CONTINUE STRAIGHT AHEAD TOWARDS THE WOODEN DOOR WITH THE BATTERING RAM IN 126; STOP ATTACKING AND HIDE BEHIND SHIELDS IN 172, OR ABANDON AND BACK AWAY, OUTSIDE OF THE ARROWS' AND THE OGRE'S REACH IN 195.

314.

I NEVER WOULD HAVE THOUGHT OLDRAK CAPABLE OF BETRAYING HIS SPECIES FOR A FEW COINS.
MONEY WAS NOT HIS SOLE INTEREST, MY FRIEND. DO NOT FORGET THAT HE TRIED TO MAKE EVERYONE BELIEVE THAT THE VAMPIRES WERE BEHIND THE MURDERS AND THE WEREWOLF DISAPPEARANCES! THIS GAVE HIM AN EXCUSE TO ATTACK YOUR LAIR. HAD HIS PLAN WORKED, HE WOULD'VE BECOME THE ABSOLUTE MASTER OF THESE WOODS...
IT'S A GOOD THING EORAS WAS THERE. WITHOUT HIM, WHO KNOWS WHERE WE'D BE NOW.
YOU ARE CORRECT, GAROLF. OLDRAK'S TROUBLES BEGAN AS SOON AS HE WENT AFTER MY APPRENTICE. I'M SO PROUD OF HIM! SPEAKING OF EORAS, WHERE IS HE?

GO TO 326.

## 315.

YOU ARE IN THE MISTS DISTRICT. IF YOU ARE IN WEREWOLF FORM, GO DIRECTLY TO 154.

173

54

26

IF YOU ARE IN HUMAN FORM, YOU CAN WANDER AROUND THE DWELLINGS, VISIT THE INN, OR GO TO THE CEMETERY. TO VISIT ANOTHER DISTRICT, GO BACK TO 180.

## 316.

77


## 317.

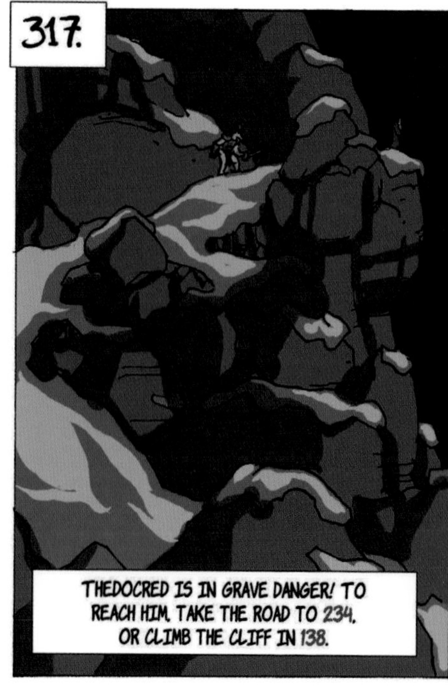

THEDOCRED IS IN GRAVE DANGER! TO REACH HIM, TAKE THE ROAD TO 234, OR CLIMB THE CLIFF IN 138.

## 318.

167

206

285

TO VISIT A DIFFERENT DISTRICT, CONSULT THE MAP IN 180.

## 319.

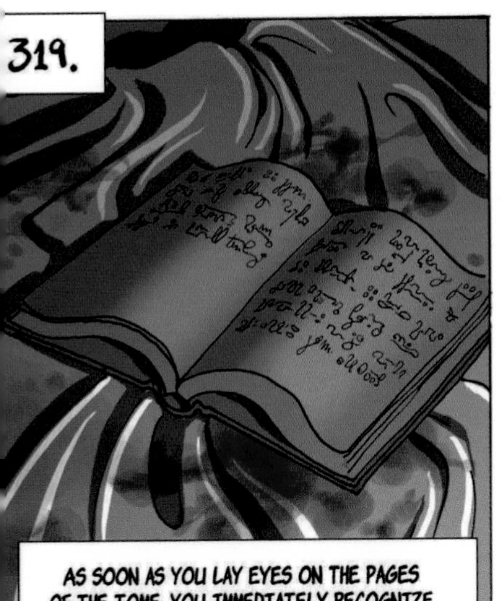

AS SOON AS YOU LAY EYES ON THE PAGES OF THE TOME, YOU IMMEDIATELY RECOGNIZE THE TONGUE OF THE WHITE BEARDS, A CLAN OF SCHOLARS WHO LIVE IN THE MOUNTAINS. YOU UTTER THE INCANTATION THAT ALLOWS YOU TO IMMEDIATELY GAIN 2 HIT POINTS! THEN RETURN TO 21.

## 320.

OH, A NEW *LOUP*! YOU LIVE IN WHITETHORN? I HAVE FRIENDS THERE, WEREWOLF FRIENDS AT THAT! I COULD INTRODUCE YOU TO THEM, IF YOU WANT. EACH NIGHT, THEY CAN BE FOUND AT THE THREE PHEASANTS TAVERN. WELL, I MUST GO NOW. I HAVE WORK TO DO...

ESMAILD CANNOT TALK TO YOU FOR LONG. GO BACK TO 127.

## 321.

82

158

THIS IS THE SEER'S TENT. IF YOU HAVE A JADE AMULET, YOU CAN VISIT HER SO SHE CAN ENCHANT IT. IF YOU DO NOT HAVE A JADE AMULET, LOOK FOR ONE AND WRITE DOWN THIS PANEL'S NUMBER SO YOU KNOW WHERE TO COME BACK LATER!

IF YOU'D RATHER VISIT ANOTHER DISTRICT, RETURN TO 180.

## 322.

146

75

50

TO EXIT THE TENT, GO TO 233.

323.

DRATS! THE CATAPULT IS TOO FAR AWAY! HELP ME PUSH IT CLOSER! MEET ME IN 130!

324.

YOU'VE GOT SOME NERVE! ANOTHER COMPLAINER? YOU DON'T LIKE MY FOOD? GET OUTTA HERE!
NOTHING INTERESTING HERE. RETURN TO THE MAIN ROOM IN 167.

325.

131
140
EVEN THOUGH TORCHES ARE HANGING FROM THE WALLS, THE HALLWAY IS DARK. YOU ARE STILL ABLE TO MAKE OUT TWO DOORS IN THE DARKNESS. YOU CAN TRY TO OPEN THEM OR GO BACK TO 152.

326.
YOUR MISSION IS COMPLETE. PEACE WITH THE VAMPIRES IS RESTORED. THEDOCRED IS SAFE, AND OLDRAK'S TREACHERY HAS BEEN UNMASKED. THE FORMER PACK LEADER WILL END HIS DAYS IN JAIL FOR HELPING SALANDAR AND THE BLACK BROTHERHOOD TO HUNT AND KILL WEREWOLVES IN EXCHANGE FOR A FEW GOLD PIECES.
NOW THAT YOU'VE UNCOVERED EVERY PIECE OF THE PUZZLE, YOU UNDERSTAND THAT THEDOCRED'S CURE FOR LYCANTHROPY REPRESENTED A RISK TO OLDRAK'S BUSINESS: FEWER WEREWOLVES TO DELIVER MEANT LESS MONEY TO EARN. SO TO PRESSURE THE OLD MAGE, SALANDAR WANTED TO KILL YOU AND BLAME YOUR DEATH ON THE VAMPIRES. SADLY FOR HIM AND LUCKILY FOR YOU, THE WOLF THAT ATTACKED YOU RUINED THEIR PLAN. THE HUNTER DIDN'T EVEN HAVE A CHANCE TO RELOAD HIS CROSSBOW. BY THE TIME HE HAD DONE SO, YOU HAD ALREADY FLED FAR AWAY.
BY DEFEATING OLDRAK, YOU'VE PROVEN YOUR COURAGE TO THE WOLVES AND YOUR LOYALTY TO THE PACK! AFTER GIVING YOU A ROUSING OVATION AND PRAISING YOU MANY A TIME, THEY HAVE DECIDED TO ELECT YOU AS THEIR NEW LEADER!
THE COLD WINTER WIND BLOWS THROUGH YOUR THICK FUR AS YOU OBSERVE THE SKY. IT IS ALREADY MORE THAN A FEW HOURS INTO THE NIGHT; IT IS TIME TO HEAD BACK HOME! YOU ARE NO LONGER A YOUNG AND QUIET APPRENTICE THAT WILL WALK THE STREETS OF WHITETHORN, BUT A PROUD WARRIOR AND A RESPECTED PACK LEADER!
THE END!

# Character Sheet

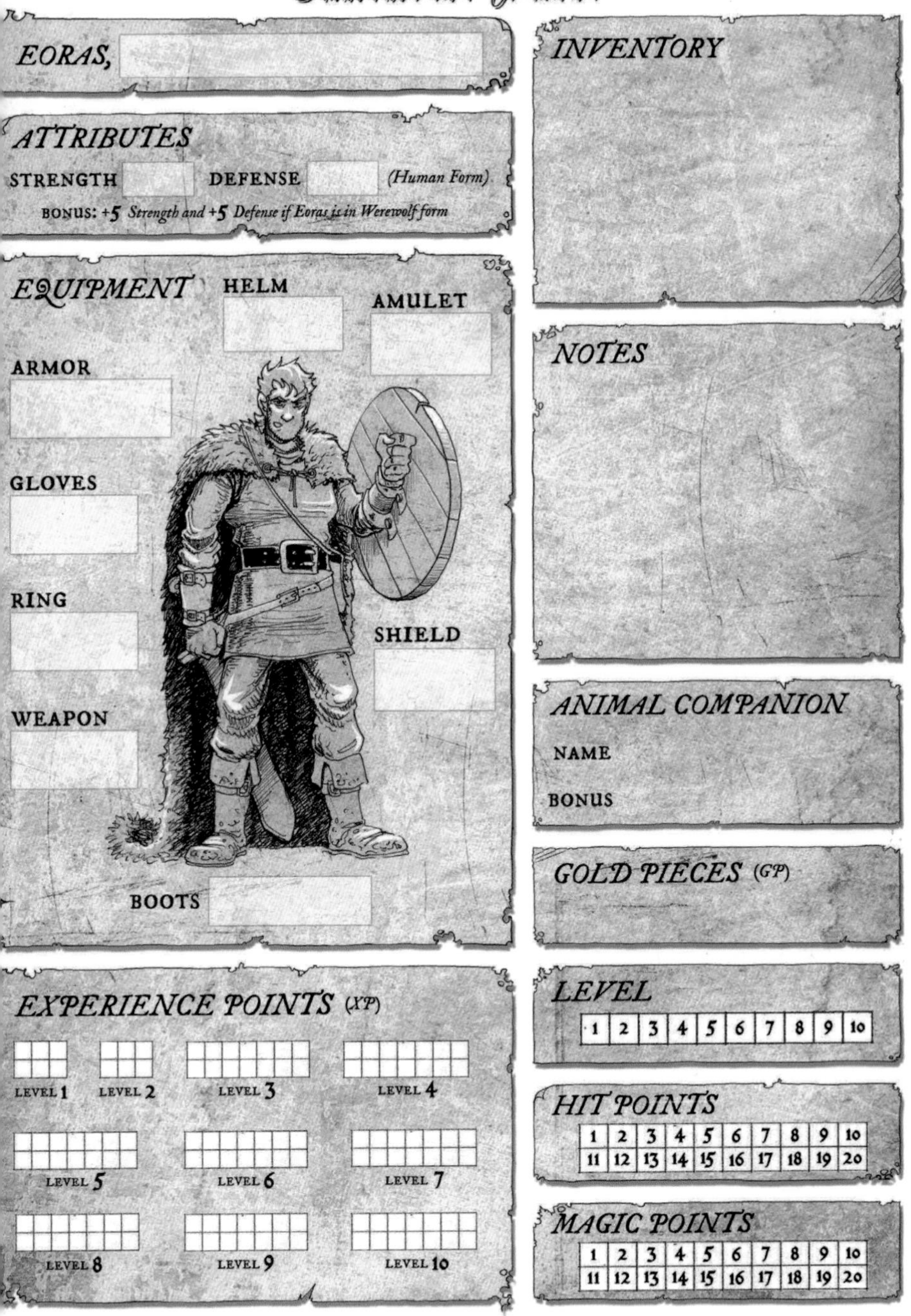
EORAS,
ATTRIBUTES
STRENGTH
DEFENSE
(Human Form)
BONUS: +5 Strength and +5 Defense if Eoras is in Werewolf form
EQUIPMENT
HELM
AMULET
ARMOR
GLOVES
RING
SHIELD
WEAPON
BOOTS
EXPERIENCE POINTS (XP)
LEVEL 1
LEVEL 2
LEVEL 3
LEVEL 4
LEVEL 5
LEVEL 6
LEVEL 7
LEVEL 8
LEVEL 9
LEVEL 10
INVENTORY
NOTES
ANIMAL COMPANION
NAME
BONUS
GOLD PIECES (GP)
LEVEL
1 2 3 4 5 6 7 8 9 10
HIT POINTS
1 2 3 4 5 6 7 8 9 10
11 12 13 14 15 16 17 18 19 20
MAGIC POINTS
1 2 3 4 5 6 7 8 9 10
11 12 13 14 15 16 17 18 19 20

# Skill Tree

Each box costs **1 Skill Point.** You may choose any box as long as it is accessible from a skill you already possess!

*NOTE: You begin your adventure with **1 Skill Point.** Choose your first profession wisely!*

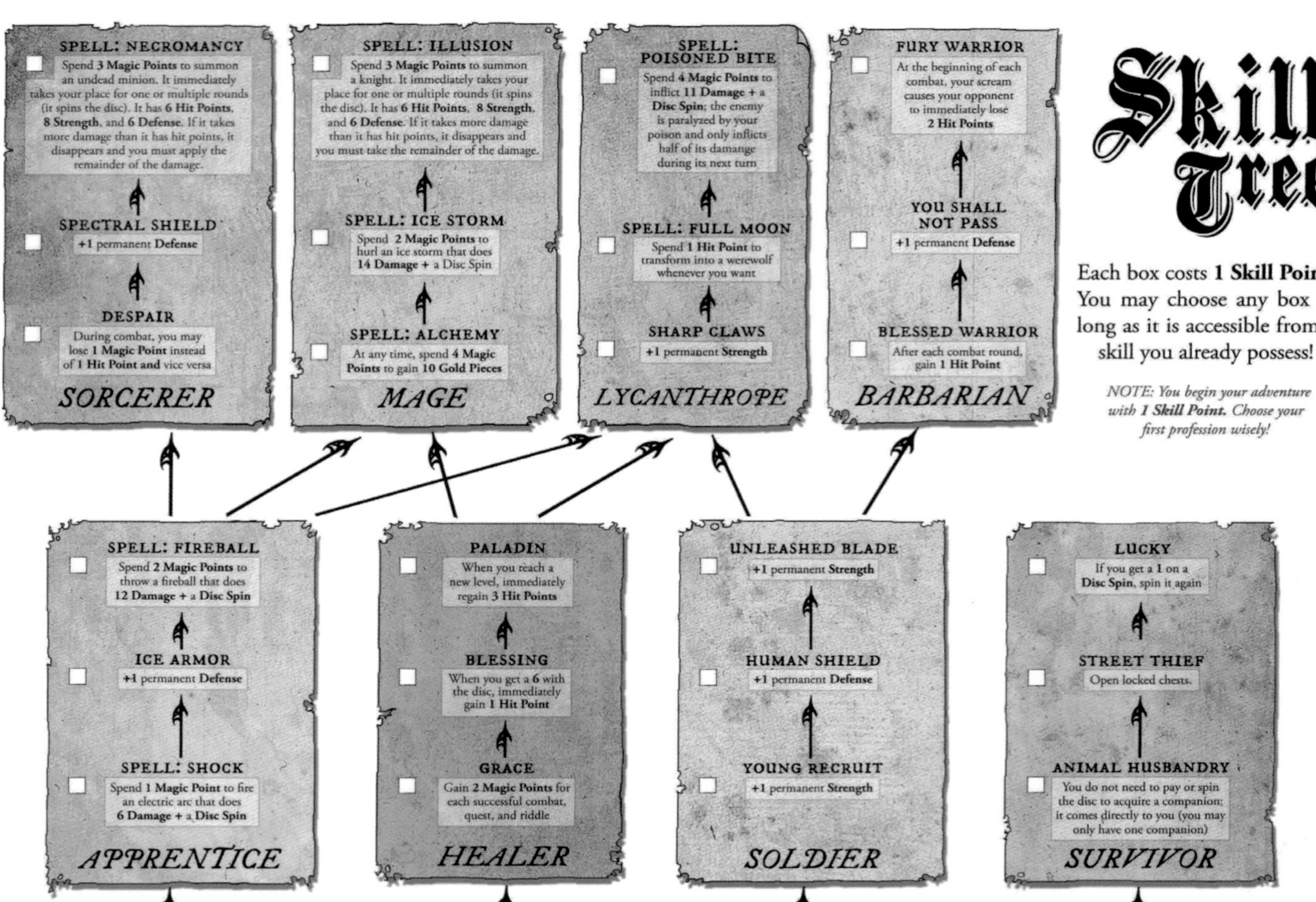

SPELL: NECROMANCY
Spend 3 Magic Points to summon an undead minion. It immediately takes your place for one or multiple rounds (it spins the disc). It has 6 Hit Points, 8 Strength, and 6 Defense. If it takes more damage than it has hit points, it disappears and you must apply the remainder of the damage.
SPECTRAL SHIELD
+1 permanent Defense
DESPAIR
During combat, you may lose 1 Magic Point instead of 1 Hit Point and vice versa
SORCERER
SPELL: ILLUSION
Spend 3 Magic Points to summon a knight. It immediately takes your place for one or multiple rounds (it spins the disc). It has 6 Hit Points, 8 Strength, and 6 Defense. If it takes more damage than it has hit points, it disappears and you must take the remainder of the damage.
SPELL: ICE STORM
Spend 2 Magic Points to hurl an ice storm that does 14 Damage + a Disc Spin
SPELL: ALCHEMY
At any time, spend 4 Magic Points to gain 10 Gold Pieces
MAGE
SPELL: POISONED BITE
Spend 4 Magic Points to inflict 11 Damage + a Disc Spin; the enemy is paralyzed by your poison and only inflicts half of its damage during its next turn
SPELL: FULL MOON
Spend 1 Hit Point to transform into a werewolf whenever you want
SHARP CLAWS
+1 permanent Strength
LYCANTHROPE
FURY WARRIOR
At the beginning of each combat, your scream causes your opponent to immediately lose 2 Hit Points
YOU SHALL NOT PASS
+1 permanent Defense
BLESSED WARRIOR
After each combat round, gain 1 Hit Point
BARBARIAN
SPELL: FIREBALL
Spend 2 Magic Points to throw a fireball that does 12 Damage + a Disc Spin
ICE ARMOR
+1 permanent Defense
SPELL: SHOCK
Spend 1 Magic Point to fire an electric arc that does 6 Damage + a Disc Spin
APPRENTICE
PALADIN
When you reach a new level, immediately regain 3 Hit Points
BLESSING
When you get a 6 with the disc, immediately gain 1 Hit Point
GRACE
Gain 2 Magic Points for each successful combat, quest, and riddle
HEALER
UNLEASHED BLADE
+1 permanent Strength
HUMAN SHIELD
+1 permanent Defense
YOUNG RECRUIT
+1 permanent Strength
SOLDIER
LUCKY
If you get a 1 on a Disc Spin, spin it again
STREET THIEF
Open locked chests.
ANIMAL HUSBANDRY
You do not need to pay or spin the disc to acquire a companion; it comes directly to you (you may only have one companion)
SURVIVOR

Disc

Dise